C000140115

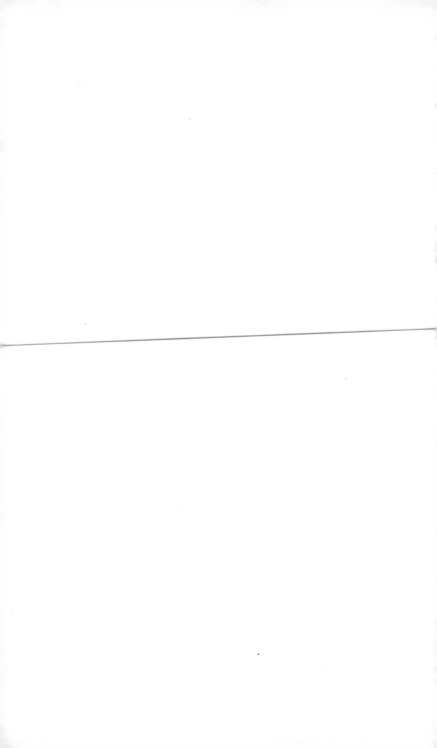

HORRORSCOPES

HORRORSCOPES:

AN ASTROLOGICAL ALMANAC

JONATHAN O'BRIEN

Constable • London

CONSTABLE

First published in Great Britain in 2015 by Constable

A CIP catalogue record for this book
is available from the British Library.

ISBN 978-1-47211-457-0 (hardback)

Typeset by Hewer Text UK Ltd, Edinburgh
Printed and bound in Great Britain by
CPI Group (UK) Ltd, Croydon, CR0 4YY

Papers used by Constable are from well-managed
forests and other responsible sources.

MIX
Paper from
responsible sources
FSC® C104740
www.fsc.org

Constable
is an imprint of
Little, Brown Book Group
Carmelite House
50 Victoria Embankment
London EC4Y 0DZ

An Hachette UK Company
www.hachette.co.uk

www.littlebrown.co.uk

#FF

@JonathanOB_
@Eggshapes
@_L_M_C_
@NotReallyNathan
@fletcherchriss
@koeman81
@_Enanem_
@CiaranM87
@DonnaGalloway_
@LauraSparling
@PFPTMillsy
@gdorean
@nonnygoggler
@vornstyle
@reggie_c_king
@ameliesoleil

CONTENTS

INTRODUCTION

Welcome to your annual Horrorscopes astrological almanac for the year ahead.

Astrology has been an inexplicable part of our lives for centuries, from the original and primitive Zodiac War thousands of years ago to the technologically reliant battlefield of the modern day. Hundreds of thousands of people look towards the stars for their daily mission, always in the hope of finally destroying the other signs and becoming the leaders of the Zodiac.

In the following pages you'll learn everything you need to know for the year to come, from when you can expect success in your personal or professional life to how to cope when you realise this year will be the same failure as the one before. You'll find out the position of various planets at the time of your birth and how this can make you more attractive to people who believe in astrology. There's even a short monthly guide so you can prepare yourself for the difficult next twelve months.

It is your astrological sign which makes up who are you are. It decides whether you respond to love like a confused child or an ancient, terrifying lothario. Your professional life can, and does, rely solely on the position of Saturn at any given moment (which is far more comforting for you not getting that promotion than the fact that you simply don't deserve it).

Every single person on the planet is unique to within twelve personality types. We hope that each and every one of you (out of twelve) can find something within these pages. Except for Libra, but you'll find out about that in July.

Good luck in the year ahead. You're all going to need it.

Jonathan O'Brien
Astrologer
Soul searcher
Dream diviner
Billionaire

PREDICTIONS FOR LAST YEAR

I described last year as one of transition mostly due to the collision of Mars, Jupiter and Venus and the ensuing destruction of Earth. It was to be a particularly difficult year for Librans, who would find that the new planetary alignments changed their personality type from bold, caring and ambitious to burning, pain-filled and dead. Unfortunately, this prediction was an incorrect reading from an experimental Astral Moon Unit Peace chart which we have since found to be faulty. This year, however, I assure you that no such mistakes will be made.

I also predicted that a strong and beautiful female Sagittarius would meet a small, mild and nervous male astronomer (Libra). The two were supposed to fall in love and indulge each other in all of their possible sexual fantasies but the number you gave me wasn't recognised and the last time I saw you on the street you didn't seem to hear my shouts across that busy road. It isn't certain where this particular reading went wrong but I'm sure that the stars have a future in mind for us.

I described last year as one of 'disorder' and 'destruction', and this was thankfully incorrect. The world did not descend into feral chaos in May like we all expected but, instead, carried on mostly as normal. This year, however? Well, get your phones ready to film one hell of an apocalypse. Personally, I can't wait.

The Catholic Church did not declare the oldest living Tamagotchi a 'living miracle'. The Pope did not say 'Eighteen years?! Oy vey! Mine only live for a day or two at the most!' The Pope also did not denounce any Pokemon that were not part of the original 151 as 'pets of Lucifer'.

Last year's winner of *Britain's Got Talent* did not, as I suggested, 'bring a new era of love and prosperity to the British Isles'. In fact, if anything, they only made things worse. I apologise.

Your sister did not come home from hospital looking like she'd gone to stay in 'dog city'. I understand that now. But I still maintain there was no need to get so violent about it.

Boyzone did not reform with five other unknown-at-the-time boybands and create one 'giant, robotic boyband machine that will rise out of the ocean like something out of *Pacific Rim*'. However, we did correctly predict *Godzilla*, although in the end this was not 'the smash hit romantic comedy of the summer starring Jennifer Aniston as a "giant robotic boyband machine" falling in love with her ex-tour manager (played by Haley Joel Osment)'.

You did not find love. You will never find love. Love is a concept that eludes, evades and avoids you. Love is like your lost luggage on the way home from a holiday to the South of France. Which you went on alone. However, we were wrong in predicting you would go to the South of France last year. You didn't. You stayed at home.

I am fully confident that this year's predictions will yield next to no mistakes. Any mistakes that do arise will be entirely down to your decision to flout the friendly advice of the planets. They didn't have to help you out, you know. The least you could do is to do exactly what they tell you to.

QUESTIONS FOR THE YEAR AHEAD

Owing to a printing error in last year's almanac, the section called 'Send Us Your Questions for the year ahead' was replaced with a page from the philosophical quiz book *Sartre for Ten*. But no matter, we don't need you to send in your questions in order for us to respond to them. Keep an eye out for your name, because here are the answers to the questions you would have provided.

'Will the gas explosion in town hurt anybody I know? Will little Billy survive the operation? How am I supposed to afford a proper funeral during the recession?'
Mrs Bygraves, Shudderhudds.

Yes. No. And that'll be £50 to the usual address.

'Is my wife having an affair?'
Philip One Thousand, Welthrop

No, Mr One Thousand. She is not having an affair. Just keep on going out with your friends on a Wednesday night. Don't come home early. In fact, why not stay out all night? Leave time for her to have breakfast by herself in the morning. In fact, why not go away for the weekend and leave her some proper time to lie in, enjoy your comfortable bed and not have to leave in a hurry before you come home?

'I'm trying to contact my grandma who passed on last year. Can you help? Is she okay?'
Susan Susan Susan Susan Susan, Plythe

It's bad news, Susan. There is no afterlife, only the dark depths of nothing. Your grandma isn't great, and she isn't bad. She is nothing. There is nothing.

'Did I leave the cooker on at work? Got a horrible feeling that there was a bit of a gassy smell as I left.'
Mr Bygraves, Shudderhudds

Probably not. Don't worry about it. I'm sure it'll be fine.

'Am I going to meet someone special this year?'
Dustbin Hoffman

Yes, Dustbin, you will. In April you will meet a beautiful young woman in the supermarket. You bump into her trolley, you apologise. She says it's okay. You talk for two minutes but the conversation never really gets going. You walk one way towards the condiments and she walks the other way to the bread aisle. You see her two more times on that shop but you lack the courage to say anything properly to her. You never see her again. You never forget her.

'Why won't you answer return my calls? I thought we had a marvellous night together; I've never been so satisfied. I thought it was something special.'
Kelly Brook, London

I'm sorry, Kelly. I'm just too busy with Christina Hendricks and Kate Upton at the moment. Maybe I'll call you when I've got a bit of free time?

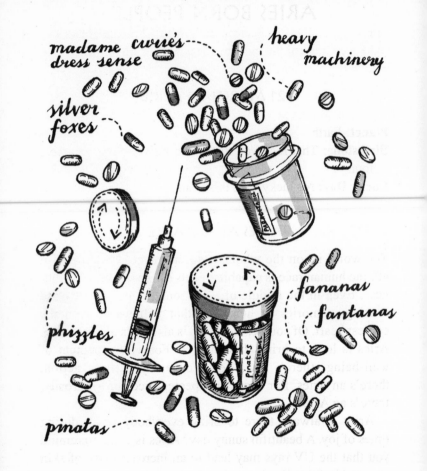

madame curie's
dress sense

heavy
machinery

silver
foxes

fananas
fantanas

phizzles

pinatas

ARIES BORN PEOPLE

21 MARCH–20 APRIL

Planet: Earth
Birthstone: That rock you threw into a river when you were four.
Lucky Day: No lucky days this year.

ARIES AT A GLANCE

The world is, on the whole, a decent place. Underneath it all, the human race is capable of acts of great love and kindness. Even in the middle of a warzone it's possible to find rousing memories of humanity that will warm even the coldest heart. Of course, the world is also a place of balance. Aries is here to bring that balance. For every moment of well-being, there's an Aries. For every selfless action, there's an Aries. For every unexpected piece of generosity, there's an Aries.

Aries is always there to bring everybody down during times of joy. A beautiful sunny day? Aries is going to remind you that the UV rays may lead to an increased risk of skin cancer. Useful to know, yes, but come on. Let's just enjoy the day.

Aries have a need for action that's almost like an addiction, but what's even more like an addiction is their need for drugs.

Anything you care to name, Aries knows how to take it and where to get it. Pills, Pulls, Silver-Foxes, Madame Curie's Dress Sense, Fananas, Fantatas, Phizzles, Pinatas, Heavy Machinery and whatever else those crazy kids are doing these days. However, with Saturn's levitation into the Pluto birocycle affecting the natural gullibility of Aries, almost everything they buy is just paracetamol coloured in with crayons by enterprising Scorpios.

Most of the other signs will approach social problems rationally. They'll take a moment to ascertain the severity of the situation and react accordingly. Not Aries. An Aries will immediately launch into an unnecessary state of panic and exacerbate the problem beyond all recognition. Haven't heard back from a friend for a day or two? Aries will assume the friend hates them and never wants to talk to them again. Partner staying out later than expected? Why, they must be sleeping with somebody else. Ironically, this attitude is often self-fulfilling and many people will simply not bother with the Aries because of their ridiculously sensitive temperament.

Aries, you're the kind of person who expects everything from everyone else and doesn't give anything back. You hold people to standards which you yourself don't meet and, what's more, you're going to tell people when they've let you down. You're the sort of person who'll 'tell it to their face' despite the fact that doing so will lead to a huge breakdown in the friendship and future communications. Don't spare somebody's feelings by keeping your thoughts about them to yourself. No, make sure to tell them exactly how much you don't like them. That's the way you deal with things. Some people think this is because you never really grew out of your teenage mindset but that's not the reason, it's all Saturn's fault. Or Jupiter's fault. In fact, it doesn't matter. It's just somebody else's fault.

You know, Aries, for somebody who hates to be kept in suspense . . .

YOUR YEAR AHEAD

With a strangulated Jupiter reaching into the face of Saturn, this may be a difficult year for you. Things you found easy last year will be a struggle. Blame others and accept no new responsibilities. Just get through it with your head down and things might get better next year.

January
1–5 One problem leads to another. Firstly, someone writes 'effect' when they mean 'affect'. So now you have a body to dispose of.
6–11 The sad thing is that nobody even notices you've had a complete mental breakdown.
12–17 Lunch goes badly today when you order Death by Chocolate for dessert and the waitress smashes your skull in with a giant Toblerone.
19–22 Your time machine proves functional but your inherent dishonesty means nobody believes you.
23–24 You see a shooting star tonight and make a wish. It's not going to come true. Your dad isn't coming back.
25–29 Check your colleagues are not only on the same page, but that they're reading the same book and can in fact actually read.

Highs: 18 On at least six occasions today, you will realise you are perfectly capable of taking the life of another human being.
Lows: 30–31 You're not as funny as you think you are.

February

1–5 You will be irritated by little things. Or 'children' as you may call them.

6–7 Jupiter in ascension, blah blah negative outcome, blah blah dog gets run over, blah blah never get over it, blah blah die under a bridge.

8–13 Your random workplace drug test comes back negative today. You'll probably want to take that up with your dealer.

14–15 Your passengers rudely wake you up with their screaming.

16–19 It turns out the unexpected item in the bagging area is your crushing sense of failure.

25–27 Darkness. A terrible despair. Blind, empty hope. The birds haven't made a single sound all day.

27–28 You'll feel frustrated today as a simple task sends you into a never-ending cycle. See Cancer for more details.

Highs: 20–24 BIRDS. THOUSANDS OF THEM.
Lows: 467–890 February feels like it's never going to end . . .

March

1 You join a long queue today only to discover it is a very tired conga line.

2–7 You get your haircut. You tell the hairdresser it's fine, but it isn't. It isn't fine.

8–12 Your plan to kill Alanis Morissette is hampered when the only thing that comes to hand is ten thousand spoons.

13–16 Did you hear about that awesome party everyone's invi . . . never mind.

20–24 Your anger is seen as a problem by others. Whereas you see your anger as the only solution.

30–31 Today, you question Gazza's insistence that he owns all of the fog on the Tyne as there are no legal documents to support his claim.

Highs: 26–27 You can't be bothered.
Lows: 28–29 You still can't be bothered.

April
1–4 It's all your fault. What is? Everything. Why? Doesn't matter. People will blame you regardless.
5–6 I can't believe you've been going out looking like that. You're a mess.
7–10 You've done well but it's finally time to lose that self-control. Let your fists fly. Set them free.
15–17 You accidentally catch a glimpse of your Google search history and realise that you need to seek professional help.
24–27 The cold hand of death is closer than ever.
28–30 You're prescribed a joke to combat your illness. It's not the best medicine. If anything, it makes you feel worse.

Highs: 11–14 Your tolerance levels are under severe stress today. Whatever happens will bother you. Even when you know it shouldn't.
Lows: 18–23 Someone tells you their problems. The best advice you can give them is to tell somebody else.

May
1–2 You receive feedback regarding an error report you sent back in 1998.
3–7 You want to go out and have a good time. But then you remember the hassle and disappointment that you usually experience.

10–17 People think you lack sympathy when it comes to their problems. Untrue. You just lack interest.

18–19 People try to be helpful for you today. You know what would be most helpful? If they stayed out of your damn way.

20–25 Feeling unwell, you Google your symptoms. Turns out you're a decommissioned fighter jet.

27–31 Like a lion you must prove you have the ability to be a leader. But killing and eating a zebra at work is apparently 'not acceptable'.

Highs: 8–9 You find a tenner in an old trouser pocket. A present from your past self.
Lows: 26 It's one of those old tenners that are no longer legal tender. Stupid past self.

June

1–5 You're not doing what you want with your life and you've no idea how to change things for the better.

7–10 Right, this is just ridiculous now. What are you doing with your life?

11–15 I don't know. I just don't know.

18–23 You have entirely pleasant and amicable conversations with a work colleague despite the fact that you hate each other's guts.

23–24 Your 'cosmic order' has been left at the nearest sorting office.

25–27 Don't worry, that cracking sound isn't your hip, it's just the last of your spirit breaking. Or you've sat on a Ryvita again.

28–30 A slug gets into your matter transporter and you become a monster. However, you win the office fancy dress competition hands-down.

Highs: 6 You spend today judging people because, well, you have nothing better to do and it makes you feel better about yourself.

Lows: 16–17 You smell nice. And you look good too. You've really made an effort. Nobody notices though.

July

1–6 You're tired. In every sense of the word.

9 Yes, your sniffing is driving the rest of the office insane.

13–15 It doesn't get any better, by the way. If anything, it's only going to get worse.

16–19 You encounter someone who seems unhappy. This pleases you.

20–24 Rules are there to be broken. So too is your heart. Only the rules don't get trampled on afterwards.

25 You pretend to ignore someone today. You know you'll eventually have to talk to them. But the delay helps you prepare.

26–31 A flirtation will make this a really interesting day for you. Unfortunately the only thing you'll be flirting with is death.

Highs: 7–8 Unfortunately, you give the impression that you're interested in someone else's dream from the previous night.

Lows: 10–13 You try to subtly check out your reflection today. You act as if you didn't but you did. You shallow mess.

August

1–3 Death would be an improvement.

4–6 Alcohol is the only friend you can rely on. It's always there for you. Never judges you. It's sad really.

8–11 The feeling of self-respect is a rarity for you. You've reached your lowest point and started to dig.

13–18 Emotionally, physically and spiritually, you need a rest. But that's not possible in this unrelenting, depressing life.

19–21 Friends will play a big part in your weekend. You've no plans so you spend the whole time watching the box sets.

22–24 AAARRRRGGGHHH! AAAARRRRRRGGGHHHH! AAAAAAAAARRRRRRGGGHHH!

25–31 You find yourself living the dream when you give a speech at your old school wearing only your underwear.

Highs: 7 Today is full of potential. Anything could happen. Though, in all likelihood, it won't.

~~Lows: 12 Another day in a world you don't understand.~~

September

1–3 You can't revisit a dream after waking up. But you're constantly waking up into the same nightmare.

11–17 You get one cat and use its cat gravity to attract another. Then use this doubled cat gravity to get more. Soon you have all the cats!

18 You calculate there isn't enough time in the day to honestly answer how you are. So you settle for a generic, time-friendly 'all right'.

19–23 Don't take any chances. Kill anything that moves.

25–27 Just try to be happy.

28–30 You shoot yourself in the head, declaring 'long live the new flesh'. It doesn't live long. Or at all. You die in the ambulance.

Highs: 4–10 It will take heroic courage for you not to react when you see someone double-click a hyperlink.

Lows: 24 People can tell you've had enough just by looking at you.

October
1–7 Your contribution to the rest of mankind is negligible.
8 According to your reading, today you have your head shaved then go for a quick run. Sounds like balderdash to me.
9–15 You used to get drunk and have a good time. Now you just feel tired and disappointed.
16–18 You'll never afford what you've been saving for. You aren't allowed nice things.
25 You forget to do something today. I don't know what, though. The planets aren't your damn diary.
26 You take things to the next level. You go from 'binge drinker' to 'full-blown alcoholic'.
27–31 Someone on the train puts their bags on the seat next to them. Don't worry, there's a special hell waiting for them.

Highs: 19 After throwing an inanimate object through your window and yelling 'HAPPY NOW?' you cry uncontrollably for several hours.
Lows: 20–24 What are you doing with your life. What does it mean. Where are you going. Why are there no question marks in this.

November
1–4 A rare planetary alignment in the cosmos has no effect whatsoever on your daily life.
5–9 You punch a loaf of bread today for calling you names. You later realise it said 'THICK CUT'.
16–20 It's easier to smile than to frown! Although, it's even easier to punch them in the face.

21 HA! Oh, the look on your face at around 4 p.m. is priceless. I wish you could see it, it's brilliant.

22–25 It's no wonder you're so alone. You're a mess.

26–27 You are bitten by a radioactive spider. But, sadly, you don't gain any superpowers. Your hair falls out and you die.

29–30 You suddenly become very conscious of your blinking pattern for no apparent reason.

Highs: 10–15 You unknowingly break the world record for the longest streak of expletives in a row without repeating a single one. Congratulations.

Lows: 28 You will feel pain and suffering. You'll be alone but you need to be strong and push to find relief. Flush the chain when you've finished.

December

1–28 Nothing. An uneventful start to the month.

29 What was that noise?

30 Oh God what's happening what is that why is it taking all those people somebody do something please somebody help them oh God it's coming for me I can feel it in my mind please help me please please please . . .

31 EVERYTHING IS FINE. DO NOT BE ALARMED. GORAX IS YOUR FRIEND.

Highs: THE ARRIVAL OF GORAX. ALL HAIL GORAX.
Lows: LIFE BEFORE GORAX. ALL HAIL GORAX.

painting

Becoming Vegetarian

growing distinctive facial hair

1936 OLYMPIC GAMES

attending the OLYMPIC GAMES

TAURUS BORN PEOPLE

20 APRIL–20 MAY

Planet: Jupiter, as long as you pay the protection money.
Birthstone: Shmirthstone.
Lucky Day: That'll be the day.

TAURUS AT A GLANCE

Taureans share many traits – and indeed the same level of popularity – with their fellow Taurus, Adolf Hitler. They are charismatic and have a strong, naturally occurring river of evil running through them like the New York sewers in *Ghostbusters 2*. Taureans reacted badly to Hitler's legacy and have gone to great lengths to ensure that it never happens again. They have decided *en masse* to keep things almost exactly the same and to never try to affect anything. Some would say this is an extreme attitude but Taureans argue that it is better to be slightly boring and obscure than to cause some of mankind's greatest atrocities.

Being so down-to-earth, Taureans look up to anyone who is slightly unconventional. That is, all non-Taureans. They long and hope to be like anyone else, even a Scorpio, but don't dare to try it. Any Taurean who shows signs of ambition or who seems to be attempting to change anything is immediately silenced by a Taurean High Council (staffed entirely by non-Taureans dressed like Winston Churchill). Taureans are banned from painting, becoming vegetarian, growing distinctive facial hair or attending the 1936 Olympic Games.

Any other star sign, if their symbol was a bull, would dress up as one at least once and enter a china shop just to see what happens. But not Taurus. Even though it would clearly be one of the all-time great life experiences, Taureans manage to resist the chaos and trouble that it might cause. Such a waste. But, then again, one day it's a light-hearted prank that would probably become a YouTube sensation, the next it's death and destruction on a worldwide scale.

Neptune makes a move on Taurus, finally ending years of speculation about its interest. But you just say no, Taurus. No planet's going to get fresh with you. You're not interested in a relationship with a planetary body that you suspect is trying to manipulate your moods and fortunes just to get you into bed. Even without the morally questionable nature of its actions, you just like Neptune as a friend. It's like a brother to you. Neptune reacts badly and moves its orbit to subtly retaliate. The other signs' usual generous nature towards you is replaced by open hostility. It's for the best, Taurus. It'll keep you in your place.

As a Taurus, you hate changes to your environment, which goes some way to explain why you haven't progressed in life. Why strive for better things when you could stay with the same old existence you've always had? Taking risks is worth it, Taurus, but it isn't for you. Not again, it's too dangerous. For a Taurus, a new carpet is about as exciting as it should get.

YOUR YEAR AHEAD

It's a complicated year for you, Taurus. Mainly because Saturn's decided to play an endless series of pranks on you.

That beautiful person you see in the street who immediately gives you their number in February, only to scream obscenities down the phone when you call them? That's Saturn messing with you. The way every single chair you go to sit on gets pulled away from you at the last minute? Saturn again. The ten-pound note on a string that moves whenever you go to pick it up? Saturn. Let's face it, Saturn's a bastard. Good luck.

January
1–4 You get the fright of your life when you realise it will only get worse.

5–13 Avoid people dressed in red tarmac. They're cycle paths.

15–18 You spend four days contemplating how a door can be a jar. Seriously, try to cut back on the drugs.

23 Despite the immaturity, you switch the light off on someone using the toilet as you think it will be funny. And you're right. It is funny.

24–26 You repeatedly tell yourself to remain calm. But that proves impossible in this idiot-filled world.

27–28 Nothing will ever be named after you. It won't even come up for discussion.

29–31 You spend your journey to work watching the person next to you play Scrabble really badly on their phone. It's very annoying.

Highs: 14 Could today be the day? No.
Lows: 19–22 The cosmos has nothing for you here.

February
1–5 You are warned on several occasions not to play Russian Roulette with a musket. It goes in one ear and out the other.

6–9 I've thoroughly double-checked and can confirm this is all you have. An empty life in which you will never be happy.

14–16 You're not easily offended. But when people are walking around oblivious that they're useless, well, something has to be said.

17–20 You assume a co-worker is an evil, sadistic scoundrel today after you lend them a pen and they never return it.

24 I'm in your bedroom right now.

25–27 It should be common knowledge that you are emotionally distant. Yet people still insist on sharing and talking to you.

28 N/A.

Highs: 10–13 You turn your email spam filter off, in the hope of some contact with the outside world.

Lows: 21–23 This chart here says that Neptune is doing a cosmic thing with Pluto which means that you will be affected in no way whatsoever.

March

1–8 There's a party in your pants and everyone's invited! But no one turns up.

9–10 Just as you build up the courage to ask the person you fancy out, they've already avoided you.

11–14 You make everyone laugh and smile. Not intentionally. But think positive.

15–17 Someone smells nice. It feels too awkward to comment. They will never make an effort again.

20 Today is a good day to showcase your brand new fake laugh.

21–25 Be careful not to take on too much at work. Otherwise you'll have no time to mess about on Twitter or Facebook.

26–27 I see travel in your future. Repeatedly, from the sofa to the drinks cabinet.

Highs: 18–19 You discover how lonely you are when you realise all pictures of you are taken at arm's length.
Lows: 26–31 There isn't enough alcohol in the world to help you forget about life. But that won't stop you from trying.

April

1 You see a car that doesn't indicate on a roundabout. It delays you by less than a second but fills you with hate.

2–10 You have an out-of-body experience today. You stand and stare at you, shaking your head at you, just like everyone else does.

16 Hahaha! Oh, I shouldn't laugh, but it's so funny. Hahaha! Just wait for 3.15 p.m. You won't find it funny, mind.

17–24 The stars have nothing for you today. They're too busy making sure Piers Morgan has a bad day.

25–27 You say the magic words but nothing happens. Try saying them again. Try crying when you say them. Try sounding more desperate.

28–29 I can't be bothered. You can't be bothered. Let's call it even.

Highs: 11–15 You should try having something other than your own sense of internal sadness for lunch.
Lows: 30 DO SOMETHING WITH YOUR LIFE.

May

1–4 You firmly press the palms of your hands into your eyes a lot. It is a short-term solution to a never-ending problem.

5 Today is brought to you by the letters F, M and L.

11–15 You can't be bothered today. Seriously. Everyone can just do one.

16–18 Someone beautiful on the bus catches you checking them out today. Slowly look at everyone else in an attempt to get away with it.

22 You wake up to discover the toothpaste tube has been squeezed from the middle. Someone will die for this.

23–25 You've put on a bit of weight. Everyone has noticed.

26–31 You secretly plant explosives in someone's camera. It's best you learn what photobombing is before more people get hurt.

Highs: 6–10 You need to start mingling in new circles. Everyone in your current circle has realised they don't like you.

Lows: 19–21 Nobody ever told you that you can actually feel your head going bald, did they? Wear a hat?

June

1 Your biggest struggle is not getting out of bed. It's finding purpose and the will to live.

9–14 If you were going to have a better life it would have already happened by now. Give up, accept your lot.

15–17 Your partner leaves you for a Henry vacuum cleaner.

22–23 You have no potential to fulfil.

23 It never ends. It's just on and on. Every day. Constant, unchanging misery.

24–29 With so many people in the world and so much going on, it's difficult to know who or what annoys you the most.

30 No, technically it isn't bestiality, but you'll never be allowed back in the butcher's shop.

Highs: 2–8 The silicon chip inside your head gets switched to overload today, resulting in mass school closures.

Lows: 18–21 You invent a new drinking game where you have to take a drink every time you remember your disappointing life. You win!

July

1–6 You have that dream again where you're naked at school. Dream, memory – what's the difference?

8–10 QUICK! PUSH THE BUTTON!

11–14 This reading is intentionally left blank. Like your hopes.

15–18 You're rewarded with extra responsibility at work. So remember – your boss has two sugars in their coffee.

19–22 I could tell you how to survive a potential fatal injury but you don't deserve to live.

24 You get two Crunchies from a vending machine today. It's all downhill from here.

25–31 You are a psychological breakdown waiting to happen.

Highs: 7 You ignore somebody shouting 'DUCK!' at you today; this is a bad move as shortly afterwards you are attacked by a giant mallard.

Lows: 23 You miss your last chance at happiness. Nice one.

August

1–5 You ask the Lord to give you strength. He answers by giving you an unhealthy addiction to steroids.

6–9 Beware the Vole of Calamity for he will smite you with his paw of torment.

11–18 You have sex and OH GOD MY EYES IT CANNOT BE UNSEEN.

21–24 The perfect smile is nothing without the perfect person to share it with. You're too miserable to have either.

25–27 NOTHING.

28 Surviving today will be a hollow victory. Death will still be following you tomorrow.

29–31 Your love life will improve eventually. There's got to be someone out there with no standards and low self-esteem.

Highs: 10 Today's going to be a brilliant day! For me, I mean – not you, your day's going to be terrible. You're eaten by wolves after lunch.

Lows: 19–21 KILL KILL KILL KILL KILL KILL KILL KILL KILL KILL KILL KILL KILL KILL KILL KILL KILL KILL KILL KILL KILL KILL KILL KILL KILL.

September

1–4 Stevie Wonder calls today just to say he hates you.

5–11 They know. That's why everyone is looking at you like that. They know what you did.

12 You feel overly pleased with yourself today when you hold a door open for a stranger.

16 You fall in love today! No, sorry, misread your chart. A threshing machine. You fall in a threshing machine today.

17–20 You finally finish Level 8-3. Eat it, Hammer Brothers.

26 A friend will offer you a shoulder to cry on. Oddly, it's a frozen shoulder of lamb.

27–30 Your mind is telling you 'no' . . . For the love of God I urge you to listen.

Highs: 13–15 Shut it, Jupiter, they'll do what I tell them to do. Give me all your money you morons! GIVE IT TO ME.

Lows: 21–25 Your partner advises you that they need more space. Why not go to the pub then?

October

1–3 Good news! You only lose half your head in the accident.

5–9 The stars say you're doomed to a lonely and boring life. But what do they know? (They know everything).

10–14 I've just rechecked your chart, hold on . . . waning gibbous, big Venus, Saturn collapsing . . . This makes NO sense.

15–17 Same as it ever was.

19–20 You can stop doing the Mobot now.

21–24 On one hand, you've succeeded in opening a portal to the Elder Gods. On the other hand, something is slowly moving its way up your arm.

26–31 You can't remember the last time you felt happy.

Highs: 18 Let's put a positive spin on this. People describe you as well-liked and popular, when your obituary is published tomorrow.

Lows: 25 Life is a journey. You did print out the AA Routefinder, didn't you?

November

1–7 Someone says 'pacifically' instead of 'specifically'. Long story short, you're sacked for violent conduct.

9–13 Your willingness to make the planets responsible for your life is one of the main reasons for your failures.

14–15 You hear someone say 'lol'. They don't laugh. They just say it. No one would blame you for hurting them.

16–19 After throwing a boomerang you struggle to figure out how it comes back. And then it hits you.

20 All Taureans die.

21–30 Still dead

Highs: 8 You buy yourself a Happy Meal today but cry uncontrollably when you realise how depressing your life is.

Lows: 16 You miss your bus, but your bus doesn't miss you. Ouch.

December

1–8 Dead. Still. Obviously.

9–14 No change. There's not much coming back from this one.

15–28 Not entirely sure what you expect here . . .

29 Hang on, something's happening. You wake up. You can feel your legs somehow. You've got an overwhelming urge for brains. Break out of your coffin and rise again. BRAINS.

30 You walk the Earth, a piece of the undead army. Commanded by GORAX, you destroy all life that's left before you. In turn he will destroy you. He will destroy all.

Highs: Your reanimation through GORAX.

Lows: The scared eyes of your loved ones as you bear down on them.

CELEBRITY READING:
DAVID CAMERON

David William Donald Cameron, born on 9 October, 1966, is a sun Libran and, like all sun Librans, no matter how hard he tries, will never miss an episode of *Coronation Street*. This will causes difficulties for him throughout the year, specifically during the upcoming economic crisis of Monday, Wednesday and Friday at 7.30 p.m. (7.00 p.m. if there's football on).

Although we cannot be sure of his official birth time, an unofficial source puts it at 6.00 a.m. which, if we accept this, gives him Libra rising, which he should seek treatment for as soon as possible before it becomes something more serious. If we don't accept his 6:00 a.m. birth time then, Lord, all sorts of other stuff could be happening, I don't know.

In addition, the moon, long a supporter of Labour, will do everything it can to make those it influences feel compassion and sympathy to David Cameron's rival. To counter this, the Conservative Party will reveal their controversial plans to destroy the moon in July. This proposal will become one of the key political battlegrounds of the forthcoming year.

In March, a group of elderly Taureans will challenge David's authority by claiming that Taureans and Librans haven't gotten along ever since a Libran someone once knew borrowed something from a Taurean and never gave it back. To counter this, David will have to embrace traditional Taurean traits like 'suddenly standing at the tops of escalators' or 'not saying thanks after someone holds open a door.' This change from his usual Libran qualities will cause him to look rude and uncaring to the voting public and he will abandon this strategy as soon as possible.

Mr Cameron will have to face potential disruption in his party thanks to an alliance between Neptune and Saturn whose positions will determine whether the half of Westminster who haven't yet read the Game of Thrones books will have the television series ruined for them by those who have read it. This will be one of the hardest challenges the Prime Minister will face in the coming year and will likely be how history remembers him.

January and December will also see David having to deal with stresses involving Saturn, the planet of obstacles, limitations and long telephone calls with banks who've unfairly charged you for slightly going over your overdraft limit.

August will see the development of wider and more serious problems throughout the world and David will need all of his powers of Libran diplomacy to make it through unscathed. His Libran powers of heat vision and super strength may also be called upon, but only as a last resort.

In December, David will unwittingly usher in the reign of GORAX THE DESTROYER and a new reign of pain and darkness the likes of which the world has never seen. Thanks, David.

LUCKY DATES TO PLAY: MONOPOLY

The first time you play Monopoly will be in the first week of January, as part of a monthly board game night at a local bookshop. You will play with your partner, your best friend and their partner. After three trips around the board you will have lost or spent all of your money. You continue to drink while they play, you get too drunk and call them all 'capitalist pigs'. Everyone knows you don't mean it but the insults bring an unfortunate edge to the atmosphere. You and your partner go home early and the next day you apologise for being so drunk. They say it's okay and you want to believe them.

The first week of February sees you playing Monopoly with the same people. This time you make it around the board four times before being bankrupted by your best friend's partner. You laugh it off, not wanting to cause the same scene as in January, but your previous actions quickly create a nervous atmosphere. You drink as they play and, although you don't go to the same lengths as last time, a few unnecessary 'quips' bring down the tone of the evening. You and your partner go home early and the next day you apologise for being so drunk. They say it's okay and you want to believe them.

March. The monthly board game night. Your partner asks if you're sure you want to go, wouldn't you rather sit in and watch a few episodes of *The Wire* instead? You say that it's fine, that it's all under control. That you won't let the evening be ruined just because you lost at Monopoly. They reluctantly agree. Your best friend, who you haven't spoken to since last month, welcomes you warmly. They kiss your partner on the cheek. Did that kiss go on a bit too long? Is that level of eye contact indicative of something else? You push it to the back of your mind. You're being ridiculous. You play Monopoly. This time, thanks to some particularly shrewd and clever play by your best friend, you're bankrupt before you can even pass 'Go' for a third time. The evening pans out as before. They play, you drink. Nobody says anything that isn't necessary for the game. You go home early, your partner stays behind. They arrive home late and don't say a word as they get into bed.

In April you decide to invite your best friend and his partner over for dinner and, to put it to rest once and for all, another game of Monopoly. The dinner goes well and the evening becomes relaxed and happy. Nobody even thinks twice when you bring out the game and start to set it up as your partner clears the table. Your friend helps as you arrange the pieces before offering to go through and lend a hand doing the dishes. Once the board is ready you go through to the kitchen to tell the others, only to find your partner and your friend kissing in the kitchen. They leap back suddenly, they apologise, they try to explain. You cannot think. You leave the house and go to stay with your parents. Their worry about you is compounded when you can only offer 'Monopoly' as the reason for your tears.

May is spent studying Monopoly. The tips, the tricks, all the ways in which you'll finally be able to beat the game. You take sick leave from work and sit in your teenage bedroom, locked into the computer screen that tells you everything you need to know. Your parents field the increasingly pessimistic phone calls from work. Your mother brings you food each night as you sit there staring at the simplistic London A–Z, a top hat in one hand and an old tattered boot in the other.

It all goes wrong in June. You go outside to get some supplies from the nearby shop and through sheer chance make friends with a local drug dealer. He offers you the occasional bit of work and within a week, while on the way to pick up £200 from a contact, you're picked up by the police and sentenced to six months in prison. You go straight to jail. You do not collect the £200.

December. You are released from prison early in the month. You have successfully destroyed the Parker Brothers factory and are now sitting in a tree outside your former friend's house. Your dog is barking. Your top hat is tattered and worn. You do not have a car. Your now ex is in the house. Your friend's partner is also there. From your vantage point you can see that they're playing Happy Families. You barge in and demand to play. Terrified, they deal the cards and, until the sirens come, you win hand after hand after hand after hand after hand.

Do YOU want to be an expert astrologer?

Do YOU want to know the daily goings-on of EVERYBODY in the WORLD just by looking at a few simple charts?

Do YOU want to attain a comforting sense of WELL-BEING and HAPPINESS and CHARGE others for a FLEETING GLIMPSE of a world that isn't filled with HATE and SPITE?

Well YOU can!

We want to teach YOU the secrets of the universe! From the movements of the planets right down to the movements of your neighbour's bowels, we can help YOU discover your inner psychic! It's been bashing at the walls, wailing and gnashing, desperate to escape the boring confines of your up until now closed mind. OPEN your mind, let out the psychic in you and into the brains of your friends and loved ones!

At our TOP SECRET training centre* we will teach you how to:

* informing the police of the location of the training centre will result in immediate dismissal.

- Read the positions of the planets and how Jupiter leaning slightly into Mars can have **fatal** effects for people who don't sign up to our course!

- Use nothing but blind hope and extensive guesswork to predict the futures of the people in the audience who've paid **hundreds of pounds** to see you!

- **Completely** abandon all sense of shame!

- Say things like **'typical Aquarius'** and make it sounds like you actually mean it!

- **Run 100m in under ten seconds!** You're going to need that sort of pace if you're going to stay ahead of the huge crowds that will one day surely gather to chase us all out of town!

But, you say, how do I sign up to this once-in-this-lifetime kind of course?!

Let us tell you! Jesus, c'mon, we're obviously building up to this. Stop interrupting. All you need to do is turn up at one of our **MANY** training centres with **£5,000** and a stamped addressed envelope containing a further **£10,000** and we'll teach you how the world REALLY works.

EDWARD TREASON – PSYCHIC AT LARGE

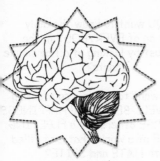

Considered one of the world's leading psychics by the people whose minds I definitely read.
They're totally thinking it. Pretty sure they're checking me out as well.

I HAVE THE POWER TO SOLVE AND HELP YOUR PROBLEMS GO AWAY. Probably.

I can help with problems involving:

- **LOVE SPELLS**
- **ANTI-LOVE SPELLS**
- **AUNTIE LOVE SPELLS.** I MEAN, COME ON THOUGH. THAT'S NOT RIGHT.
- **UNDERFLOOR HEATING**
- **CURSES**
- **TOILET PROBLEMS**
- **PROTECTION FROM UNWANTED FORCES** SUCH AS SOMEONE WISHING REALLY, REALLY HARD AGAINST YOU WHEN THEY BLOW OUT THE CANDLES ON THEIR BIRTHDAY CAKE
- **BOILER ISSUES**
- **BROKEN RADIATORS**

I have in my office documented evidence that I have given readings for various **celebrities**. There are pictures of me with that one off *Coronation Street*, no, not that one, the other one and what's his name from *Eastenders*. You know him, or at least you'll recognise his face! This list is almost endless. But it isn't endless.

ut don't listen to me, here's what some eople have definitely said about me.

'You're the real deal, and totally handsome! Let's go out for dinner sometime.' - The pretty one from *Emmerdale*.

'My partner and I are back together and desperately waiting for the day when you said we'll be happy again' - **Mr Frankford PicketPicketPicket, Leeds**

'The accuracy of your reading was incredible, now I'm afraid to leave the house.' - **Mrs 3unstarbarnable, Scotland** (I hope you're still staying indoors and sending your weekly protection cheque, Vera!)

My reputation is now, thanks to those three cast-iron testimonials, beyond all doubt and **anyone who says otherwise is lying and I will fight them.** My entire purpose in life is to help you to improve your life, one premium rate phone call at a time.

CALL THE USUAL NUMBER TODAY!

GEMINI BORN PEOPLE

21 MAY–21 JUNE

Planet: TBD
Birthstone: Some mud.
Lucky Day: Any of the days where you somehow manage not to get punched.

GEMINI AT A GLANCE

Geminis are like society's appendix. We've evolved past the need for them, they don't do anything any more and, if we wanted, we could remove them without any significant effect on our lives. Geminis do not reach the minimum height requirements for the rollercoaster of life.

Geminis are more interested in the accumulation of knowledge than that of money so it's a wonder how they still know so little. Did you know that a Gemini has never won a major UK television quiz show? A Gemini's memory retention is awful and, if you have one on your pub quiz team, you'd be better off without them.

Geminis are the sort of people who expect to get a pay rise at work just because they turn up on time and barely do the job that's expected of them. No overtime, no extra effort, all the expectations. When they don't get what they want, they'll cause enough of a fuss until they do get it and so the cycle continues.

They will, when it's raining, hit other people with their umbrellas and not even notice. They don't wait for people to get off the London Underground before they get on. They are rude to people who work in call centres and don't even realise how horrible they are being.

As a Gemini, you embody all the traits of love, compassion and losing your job because of gross incompetence. No other sign even comes close to your ability to completely miss the point of any simple task given to you. Who knew that photocopying a sheet for Jones in cubicle twelve would lead to the company losing almost half its value on the stock market? You are, in no positive way whatsoever, an economic marvel.

Because of your uselessness, you will find it hard to find love with anybody but another Gemini. Unusually, the star sign of two Geminis' offspring is decided by genetics rather than date of birth. If you and another Gemini have a child, that child will also be a Gemini. Sure, on paper it might be a Leo or Pisces, but its DNA will be that of a quiet and unassuming loser who rarely gets anything right. Please, Gemini, think of the child. Is that really a life you want to be passing on to them?

The important thing to remember, Gemini, is that it's not that the stars can't help you. They just don't care. They are interstellar bodies travelling through the glorious expanse of space and you are nothing but a speck on the windscreen of the galaxy, ready to be wiped away by the windscreen wiper of fate. If Jupiter wanted to it could make a deal with Mars to hand you the winning lottery numbers. But it won't. It never will.

YOUR YEAR AHEAD

Your areas of interest in the year ahead will be: body image, trains, the theme tunes to children's television programmes from the 1990s, terrible first dates, the second series of *Monty*

Python's Flying Circus, how many tears it takes to fill a milk bottle (you will have plenty of opportunities to learn this one), Greggs the baker, the amount of times you can text someone before giving up on receiving a reply, empty bottles of whisky, high bridges, long falls, loud noises and the emergency services.

January

1 Your New Year's resolution is 1280 x 720.

2–6 A clip of you slipping on the ice and falling badly gets 12 million views on YouTube.

7 Lady Luck will smile upon you today. Just don't let Lord Luck catch you winking back at her whilst staring lasciviously at her bosom.

15 You realise today that there is little scarier than someone screaming the theme tune to *Beadle's About*.

16 As you sit and watch flakes fall through the air, you decide that the ice-cream van shouldn't have taken that corner at such speed.

17–25 What doesn't kill you will only make you wish it had.

26–31 The voices in your head are loudly suggesting you do bad things. My advice would be to do what they say.

Highs: 8 For you, it's cat day! For everyone else, it's feel a little disturbed by your cat costume day.

Lows: 9–14 Still aiming for that promotion? Look at you, working so hard for no reason. And working so badly as well. Bless.

February

1–5 You realise that the beautiful stranger on the train is not in love with you like you hoped. You should never have spoken to them.

6–8 Somebody steals the silver lining from your cloud. Still, every cloud has . . . oh, oh yeah. Sorry.

9–11 An old relationship gets back on track as your stalker is released from prison.

12–14 DEATH DEATH DEATH DEATH DEATH DEATH DEATH DEATH DEATH DEATH DEATH DEATH . . . no, wait, I mean LIFE! Hold on, sorry, no, DEATH.

16 You're excited when you discover someone has a secret crush on you. Tomorrow, though, they'll send you clumps of their hair.

22 Today you realise you haven't experienced cold like this since your parents used to look at you.

23–27 Listen. Can you hear that? No? That's odd. We should still be able to hear it. I think it's escaped. Grab something heavy.

28 You once again get away with doing the bare minimum today.

Highs: 15 Mars and Jupiter team up to take your wallet today. Mars grabs your arms, Jupiter gets the goods. You don't bother reporting it.

Lows: 17–21 PILLOW FIGHT!

March

5 They say Christmas comes only once a year but not today! It's Christmas again! Merry Christmas! CELEBRATE IT NOW.

6–10 You find the long-lost city of cats (there is no long-lost city of cats, it's a metaphor for love [love is a metaphor for death]).

11–14 As it's now March, it's a chance to reflect on all you've achieved so far. Not much, is it?

15 Your life today is like that thing Tom Hanks said in a movie. There's a snake in your boots.

16–19 Owing to a gravitational anomaly, Mars is closer than usual. Doesn't concern you though. You still have a terrible time.

20 Uh-oh. You can swim, right?

25–31 Two words: porcupine calamity.

Highs: 1–4 Don't make any long-term plans.
Lows: 21–24 A tragic disfiguring accident has some advantages, as you now look exactly like your passport photo.

April

1–4 A military coup means you lose your position as Cat President. You'd be annoyed but their little uniforms are so cute!

5 Today, your eyes will be bigger than your belly! Seek urgent medical advice.

6–8 You find yourself locked in my . . . I mean, a stranger's closet. Don't shout for help, nobody will hear you.

9 Tragedy today when you spill some Vicks VapoRub on yourself and get eaten by a rogue koala.

10–16 Fame at last! You contract a disease so rare that they name it after you.

17–20 Once again, you fail to get the coveted Employee of the Month award. This time, the fax machine beat you to it.

26–29 When you finish struggling through the obstacles of life to gain acceptance, you'll still die alone and miserable.

Highs: 21–25 You find God, and claim the £5 reward.
Lows: 30 Be wary of parsley. Your lucky element is xenon.

May

1–4 'New haircut?' your colleagues ask. You haven't had a haircut. Why would they think that? WHAT'S GOING ON?

5–7 If I said you had a beautiful body would you hold it against me? Actually, moot point.

8 In life, everyone gets one opportunity for true happiness. Today marks the one-year anniversary of the day you missed yours.

9 Meetings will take up a lot of your time today. Mostly with your solicitor discussing your rights.

16 You see a handsome man on the bus start a conversation with a beautiful young woman. You will never be them. Never.

18–25 After taking more mushrooms and attacking the toilet with a wrench, you start to regret taking your life choices from Mario.

26–31 When making life decisions, you are advised to think about yourself. But that only makes you sad.

Highs: 10–15 You suffer the effects of severe smoke inhalation but don't worry, you're soon cured.

Lows: 17 Today you find the Lost Sword of Lothar! Then another one. And, later, another. Boy, Lothar lost a lot of swords.

June

1 The stars say you magically transform into a celebrated Russian author today but I think it's a bit of a Tolstory.

2–6 They say everyone is their own harshest critic. They are of course wrong, as you find out at today's performance appraisal.

7 The huge spider that lives under your bed climbs into your mouth this evening, to lay her eggs.

18 The spotlight is firmly on you today. The police helicopter will catch you eventually.

19 It's like the blind leading the blind at work today, as your company hires a blind man to be your boss, and you go blind.

20–24 You try to send a message to a Native American tribe, and the whole thing goes up in smoke.

25–30 Your unreasonable expectations in life are matched only by your assumption that you deserve something more.

Highs: 8–14 You're disappointed to discover a friend has started taking drugs. All your best ones, too.

Lows: 15–17 It's remarkable how much your life resembles a sitcom. Except instead of canned laughter, you get bottled crying.

July

2 This morning, you accidentally (don't ask how) swallow a heavily sedated rat. The rest of the day is a waiting game.

3 The influence of Mars today helps you work, rest, and play.

4–10 After far too long, you finally forget who Little Mix are.

11–14 Don't do what the voices tell you. The voices are not your friends.

15–18 Life is but a lava lamp, and we are all just blobs of wax. On an unrelated note, you really need to lay off the acid.

24 You play your favourite game, called 'go to work and try not to cry'. You lose 30 minutes before the office closes. So close!

25–31 You attempt typing the third, fifth and eighth characters of a password without counting on your fingers. You're only human.

Highs: 1 Jupiter pulls your hair and runs off giggling today. Bullying or something more? It's bullying. They'd never like you, speccy.

Lows: 19–23 Devote your energies to human psychology. Then when it all goes wrong you'll be well versed to plead insanity.

August

1–9 You continually inspire people to greatness. One look at you, and they'll do anything in their power to avoid becoming like that.

10–14 Is this love you're feeling or have you just not made it to the bathroom in time? It's the latter, isn't it?

15–17 A picture says a thousand words. In your case those words are more garbled screams of horror and fear.

18–20 Another good day's work as a freelance sound recordist. Business is booming.

21–22 Bad luck comes in threes. As you're attacked in a mobile phone shop.

23 You lend a colleague your pen today and watch in horror as it enters their mouth. The person will never be your friend.

27–29 They said it was them, not you. But actually it was the movement of the planets that slowly made them stop loving you. And your face.

30 Remember that a stranger's just a friend who's going to tie you up with the others one day and leave you to die.

Highs: 24–25 Your clown costume is terrifying and I have no idea why you thought it would be suitable for an office environment.
Lows: 26 You get to the bus stop just as the bus is arriving. The smug sense of satisfaction is the best feeling you have all day.

September

1 You find a baby, pick it up and all day long you have good luck. Hold on, that's not right. Put that baby down, you monster!

2–5 What really bores you is repetition, i.e. when people repeat themselves you find it boring. A repetitive horoscope will bore you.

6–9 You finally realise that 'the Lord giveth and the Lord taketh away' is from the Bible, and wasn't written by someone with a lisp.

10 The cosmos, which monitors your every move, has started to get really bored.

15–18 You have a bad case of the Monday Morning Blues, and the supermarket is all out of Smurf poison too.

19 Someone threatens your life today. I know who it is. But if I tell you, I'd have to kill you.

20–25 This is all you can expect from life. Maybe a different job at some point, maybe different friends. Variations on a boring theme.

Highs: 11–14 You develop a large gay following. If you run fast, they won't catch you.

Lows: 26–30 You destroy downtown Tokyo in an effort to be more like Godzilla.

October

1–5 After accidentally erasing all server data at work, your attempts to 'blame it on the boogie' don't work.

6–11 You believe you bemuse a French mime artist today because he has a blanc look on his face.

12 You yourself find words reading in the order wrong.

13–16 An argument at a bingo hall leads to an afternoon of wild passion, followed by an evening at hospital.

17 A bad day for you as your lucky chimney sweep dies in a chimney sweeping accident.

18 You yawn today in front of a deaf man and he thinks you're screaming.

19–21 Sometimes you wanna go where everybody knows your name. That place just happens to be Hell.

28–31 OH GOD DO SOMETHING I'M SO BORED OF PREDICTING YOUR DAILY NOTHING.

Highs: 22 A mixture of fear and arousal this morning when your Peter Andre poster kisses you back.

Lows: 23–27 You say 'potato', you say 'tomato'. You have Vegetable Tourette's.

November

1–3 Life gives you lemons, you make lemonade. Disgusting, lonely, divorce-causing lemonade.

5 You find a penny, pick it up, take it home, melt it down and add it to the terrifying figure of your copper wife.

6 You get angry when someone says the C-word. It's far too soon to be thinking about Christmas.

16–25 Your girlfriend dumps you, as she says you're insensitive to the fact that she has alopecia. Her loss.

26–29 You're from the University of Life! Who cares if you haven't got a single qualification asked for on that job application? The interviewer, that's who.

30 You realise today that you're not even creative enough to think inside the box.

Highs: 4 This morning, like every morning, you repeatedly hit your bike with a hammer. Maybe one day you'll break the cycle.

Lows: 7–15 You step into the quantum leap accelerator and vanish.

December

1–31 High up in the mountains, you relax. This spiritual retreat was worth it. You feel refreshed. You feel happy. At the end of the month you pack your bags and look forward to the future. You have a feeling it's going to be a wonderful year.

Highs: The entire month. Just wonderful.
Lows: Nothing. It's been perfect. Nothing can ruin this good mood.

bums legs arms

ornaments

decorations

Cancer, you like to
PINCH STUFF

CANCER BORN PEOPLE

22 JUNE–22 JULY

Planet: Earth?
Birthstone: The last Chaos Emerald you never managed to collect.
Lucky Day: Ha!

CANCER AT A GLANCE

Some famous Cancers include: Bowel, Testicular and Breast. Don't be afraid of personal growth, but avoid being detected early. There's a reason cancer is called cancer, Cancer. You are a deadly growth that's been slowly destroying mankind for centuries. A mass of dead cells that multiply until it's too late to stop. Did you know that the person who invented cigarettes was a Cancerian? I don't know if that's true, I just made it up, but it wouldn't surprise me. It feels right somehow, doesn't it? You sicken me, Cancer.

Cancer's personality type is right in plain sight. It's simple. Cancer is the crab, and you like to pinch stuff. This is why so few people invite you round to their houses anymore. There are only so many ornaments and decorations you can take before people start to get suspicious. But it's not just inanimate things that you like to pinch, oh no. Bottoms, chests, legs, arms . . . no part of the body is safe. You're a pest, Cancer, and everybody knows it.

Also, continuing the link to crabs, you have crabs. An endless supply of them. Cancers are the Western world's primary source of crabs. It's a medical mystery; thousands of remedies have been attempted but none of them work. Live with it, Cancer, and remember that you're legally obliged to tell your partner.

However people often fail to realise that Cancerians care deeply about the world and everybody in it. Because they don't. When pressed, they couldn't give a monkey's about anyone. They're just in it for themselves and will push aside anybody who gets in their way.

Cancerians are considered to be the most spiritual sign of the zodiac but some say it's best to keep an open mind. One man's 'voice of Gaia' is another's 'chemical imbalance of the brain'. And while the first man has spent years in the mountains of Tibet learning how to speak directly to the Earth, the other man has twenty years' experience in neuropsychology, specialising in schizophrenia and other disorders of the brain. The second man, of course, is insane. Because this is a book about astrology, the one true science.

Cancers want nothing more than to feel love but this is unlikely thanks to their bizarre physical appearance. I'm not saying that appearance is the only thing that people look for in a relationship. There are plenty of other reasons that cause two people to fall in love. There's kindness, generosity, a good sense of humour or a unique skill that really sets someone apart from the rest. These are all things that can go beyond mere physical attraction. Cancers have none of the above qualities or, for that matter, any other redeeming features. Cancers can expect a life of misery which, thanks to astrology, they can blame on the movement of the planets rather than their own lack of effort. Thanks, Mars!

Cancers are most commonly found under bridges, in doorways, shouting at people in the park or smelling of sandwiches on the back of the bus.

YOUR YEAR AHEAD

It's one to forget, to be honest. Jones in marketing gets the promotion you thought you were due. Jones in marketing seduces both your wife and Stacey the intern at the office party. Jones in marketing sounds brilliant. What sign is he? The sign of a WINNER, that's what he is. You? You're a crab.

January
1 Today, the time and location of your birth will affect outcomes, but not in the way you would logically expect.
2–7 A figure from your past reappears: the telephone number of your childhood home. No one lives there now.
11–15 Neptune has moved into your sign's first House. Yet, if you stave it with a brick, you get done for assault. How's that fair?
16–19 Love is in the air! You should open the window and freshen the room before your partner returns from the weekend at her mother's.
20 Your sense of humour is especially acute today. You will be able to detect people laughing at you from several feet away.
21–26 Your day takes a violent turn for the worse quite early on.

Highs: 8–10 I wouldn't touch it; it looks like it will spread to other damp areas.
Lows: 27–31 You're feeling confident today, and rightly so. You have no idea what you did last night so have no need to feel ashamed. Yet.

February

2–3–4 Hit it!

5–9 It's cold outside, but not as cold as your heart. It'll be warmed by a sudden need for defibrillation. Which won't be successful.

10–14 You've always known the love of your life: the abstract concept of 'utter loneliness.' Have fun you two and don't stay out too late.

19–22 You either have a problem with cancer or with crabs. It's unclear which. Maybe both. Cancer of the crabs? No, that's nonsense. Dunno.

23 You're not quite feeling yourself today. Your coordination is a bit off. Move your hand a yard to the left. Grab whatever that is.

24–26 You wake up from the deepest sleep you've had in years. And earlier than expected. Don't squirm, let me stitch you to the others.

27–28 An annoying circular process will get on your nerves. See Aries to find out more.

Highs: 1 A once-per-millennium misalignment offers a rare day of Free Will. I doubt you'd know what to do with it. Waste it on sweeties?

Lows: 15–18 Don't listen to others when they tell you how important change is. They say it's for a cup of tea, but they'll spend it on drink.

March

1–4 Humour could alleviate an awkward social situation. Although putting breadsticks in the corpse's mouth, like tusks, may not work.

5 Mars's position makes you irresistible to the opposite sex but you won't realise as Jupiter's has destroyed your self-confidence.

6–15 Don't believe everything you hear. What sounds, at first, like a tempting invitation is really the German word for six.

16 Uranus will play a central part in your love life today, as will humorous misunderstandings.

17–22 They call Cancer 'Britain's biggest killer' and the Zodiac Wars haven't even started yet. One year from now will be a glorious day.

31 Before you even get to work you've already had enough of it.

Highs: 12 Pluto, hell-bent on revenge, is heading straight for us today but it's so small that nobody notices. Good one Pluto. Loser.

Lows: 23–30 You think there are some things you can't change, but you can and should, as you are starting to smell a bit.

April

1–3 Some shy away from the C-word, Cancer. Explain you mean your star sign and they will use the C-word readily. About you. Behind your back.

4–9 You're always looking back! Quit living in the past, in a pre-rational age where people believed stars could predict future events.

10–12 It's time to take what's yours! Who cares if they're the ones who found the forgotten Aztec map? You deserve the spoils!

25 Nobody said it would be easy. If they had, you'd not have turned down the role of the clown and you'd be famous now, not Tim Currie.

26–29 Death is too good for you. But so is life. This is a quandary. Give me more time. Just don't move. That'll do for now.

30 One day you'll wake up and realise that you've got nobody left to blame but yourself.

Highs: 13–17 Now's the time! You're finally going to break out of your humdrum routine and do something with your life! No, no you won't . . .
Lows: 18–24 It's a shame. Your face was so pretty and, now . . . well, just look at it. You should never have goaded that nun.

May
1–2 You think of transferring university courses to study the animation of Walt Disney but decide not to as it's a bit of a Mickey Mouse degree.
3–7 A reference to Duane Eddy will be wasted on younger readers.
14–20 A fatal car crash proves that there are indeed only two certain things in life. Death and taxis.
21–29 You decide to take a risk today by putting your iPod on shuffle. And to think everybody says you're boring. You'll show them!
30 You try not to yawn today. You fight the urge. But you will fail.
31 Today is brought to you by the words 'please', 'God', 'no', 'don't', 'kill' and 'me'.

Highs: 3 An unexpected solar eclipse makes a great opportunity to pickpocket a nearby old woman.
Lows: 8–14 No surprises in store for you I'm afraid. I wish you were more interesting, if only for my sake. I don't care about you.

June

1–6 It's make or break time, Cancer. Or both, if you're having an omelette.

7 You find a magical-looking lamp but nothing happens when you rub it because magic isn't real.

11–14 The new guy in your team's odd. You make reluctant bedfellows. But, if the boss asks you to do something for his camera, you do it.

16–17 You wake to a heart-touching scene, as you come round from anaesthetic during cardiac surgery.

18 Today, they will come for the Sagittarians and you will not speak out because you are not a Sagittarius.

19–30 You have to look deeper into your heart to know what you truly want. No. Deeper. Dig right through. Through the pain. Deeper.

Highs: 8–10 The movement of Earth into the house of Sun Ra results in the drone band using the dead jazzman's synth on a new record no one buys.

Lows: 15 Today you discover a huge news story about scissors but aren't allowed to run with it.

July

1–6 An old enemy comes out of the woodwork, spoiling the funeral for everyone.

7 Your obsession with the person across the road goes to new heights today when a ladder gives a better view through their window.

8–15 The Tarot pack reveals Death as your card. This is normally a sign of change. Not for you, though. For you it means death.

17–22 Your mum's so fat her gravitational field pulls Jupiter out of alignment, changing your reading dramatically. Not a good few days for you.

24 You accidentally drink a friend's coffee today. You have no problem with coffee; it's just not your cup of tea.

25–31 Waking up before noon is no way to live your life.

Highs: 16 You bring out the best in others today, starting with their still-beating hearts.

Lows: 23 Fresh information ensures your financial security. Their PIN is 4921, I get half.

August

1–2 YOU TRICK EVERYONE INTO THINKING YOU'RE ANGRY TODAY BY TYPING IN CAPITAL LETTERS.

3–8 Your love life takes a turn for the better when you realise that they didn't spot you in the bushes after all.

9–12 People say black cats are unlucky but, for you, the freak piano accident today is the true cause of bad luck.

16–19 You meet someone at a coconut shy. You really hit it off.

23–27 A beautiful person asks you out at work. At least, they would if you had a job. Or any attractive qualities.

28–31 Remember: 'How stupid can you be?' is *not* a personal challenge.

Highs: 13–15 You throw your recycling into the 'general waste' bin and worry for the rest of the month that someone's going to shout at you.

Lows: 20–22 The house of Mars on Orion's Belt indicates that a Leo in the cusp of Pluto will . . . oh, forget it, I don't know what I'm talking about.

September

1–4 Your wife goes on holiday to the Caribbean after your incessant crying made her feel like she had no choice.

5–9 Your robot army is nearly complete! You just need a bit more cardboard for some finishing touches. Then they'll see! THEY'LL ALL SEE.

10–13 You get fired from your job in a circle-making factory because you kept cutting corners.

14–16 You stop reading a newspaper story about human rights abuse in order to look at the funny picture of a dog on the next page.

17–23 None of your plans for the future will work out the way you want. Just accept what you have, it'll never change. This is it. Forever.

26–30 You finally find the person you've been looking for. But they're not looking for you.

Highs: 24–25 You finally manage to remember all the moves to the Macarena.

Lows: 10 You send a chain letter to twelve friends but your luck doesn't improve. What did you expect? Astrology is your friend. Your only friend.

October

1 Jupiter in ascension while Mars descends is just the start of tonight's rare planetary orgy. Get a telescope and some tissues.

2–5 You visit a friend's house. They have a shower curtain so gaudy you cannot bring yourself to ever speak to them again.

7–14 An incident with office stationery leaves you exhausted. This is a sign that you must never become a lion-tamer.

15–18 Death comes to all. But *especially* to you.

19–24 You have a flashback to your previous life. Even as an ant you were a crushing failure.

Highs: 28–30 A motorcycle stunt goes badly wrong when you find your partner in bed with it two hours before the show.

Lows: 6 Cancers are actually 10% less likely to get cancer itself but, conversely, are 100% more likely to be killed by a bus today at 4 p.m.

November

1–7 Your *Crystal Maze*-themed date goes badly wrong when you fail a basic challenge and get locked in the Friend Zone.

8–10 The conjunction of Venus and Pluto today makes you late for work. But try telling that to your boss.

14–19 Millions of people will die because of your actions.

26–27 You see a fight on the street. You don't help. You just watch with inhuman disinterest before moving along.

28–30 You discover that you don't know much about work colleagues on a personal level. This is because you don't care about their lives.

Highs: 11–13 You come home to find Simon Cowell in your house. 'This is my house now,' says the TV and music mogul. 'Get me a sandwich,' he says.

Lows: 20–25 You want to like people. But they make it so fucking difficult.

December

1–3 The doors of your advent calendar reveal Cthulhu, lord of darkness. I told you you should've left that creepy calendar in the woods.

4–6 Your wife tells you she's pregnant with the Lord's child. It's probably not true but you can't bear the alternative. Believe her.

7–12 Something's starting to feel wrong. Your dog's acting strange.

13–20 You don't see any insects anywhere. In fact, where have all the birds gone?

21–28 The electricity isn't working? Stay calm, it'll be under control soon, surely?

29 That noise. That awful noise.

30 Oh God. What's that? What's it doing to those poor people?!

31 EVERYTHING'S FINE. HUG GORAX. HUG GORAX IN THE MOUTH.

Highs: Gorax.
Lows: Everything before Gorax.

CELEBRITY READING: THE QUEEN

Queen Elizabeth II was born Princess Elizabeth Alexandra Megatron Chutzpah Look I Really Don't Think We Can Have Megatron As A Middle Name No Don't Include That Last Bit Let's Just Lose All That And Put Mary No Don't Sign It Oh Balls on 21 April 1926 at 2.40 a.m. At the time of the Queen's birth, the zodiac sign of Aries was rising over the western horizon, a bottle of vodka in its hand and belting out its best Diana Ross impression. It is for this reason that the Queen is a big fan of Rod Stewart although, to be honest, nobody is entirely sure why.

With the moon in Libra the Queen is calm, prepared and doomed to wear a series of increasingly ridiculous hats at many state occasions. As the moon waxes and wanes, her hats undergo a similar transformation. Some people would call the Queen a victim of 'werehats' but such a concept is ridiculous and obviously doesn't fit in with the clearly defined paths that the numerous celestial bodies have put in place for the Queen with their swirling about and that. The Libran moon bestows a sense of calm on Elizabeth II; she is level-headed and can remember the words to every TV programme she has ever seen or, indeed, hasn't seen. Or can she? She can.

In the Queen's chart, Mars boldly struts around as if he owns the place which, as a matter of fact, he does, having won Buckingham Palace in a centuries-old bet with Pluto. This is a 'tribute year' for the Queen in which she must willingly sacrifice one of her loyal corgis to the Red Planet. There is literally no other reason for her to have those ridiculous dogs. In the second half of the year, Mars will be offered one of her canine companions and it will take it to join the many others it has consumed over the years. Soon Mars will have enough royal corgis with which to populate his planet with his own royal family. Then we'll see. Then we'll all see.

The next twelve months will see the Queen relax a bit and maybe hand over a small sliver of the power which she has clung onto all these years like a child who knows it's only got a few months left before it has to get out of the pram and be forced to walk while its younger sibling gets pushed around. But not to Charles. Never to Charles. If Charles takes power then the pact with Mars will be broken and the Palace will be destroyed by the Queen's once loyal corgi-hordes. Charles must never know the secret of his birth, under an Aquarian equinoxical tangent, and the disastrous events leading up to it. I've said too much.

There will be some slight indications of health problems but nothing that a quick injection of the blood of the poor won't fix. In the latter half of the year, the Queen will evolve into her final form, Mecha Queen, and lead the United Kingdom in a doomed battle against GORAX THE DESTROYER. Everyone will perish.

Practitioners of **homeopathy** believe that the causes of a disease in healthy people will also cure sick people suffering from the same disease. That by exposing the body to what originally made it ill will, in effect, cure the body. That by diluting a substance in water, the water itself takes on some of the properties of the original substance. By careful administration this solution can then act as a genuine medical cure.

NONSENSE

This approach is clearly absurd and, what's more, has never been shown to be more effective than a simple placebo. But not because homeopaths are incorrect. No. They are more correct than they know except in their choice of water they have simply chosen the wrong elemental element as their means of delivery.

When homeopathy chose to fight illness with illness, this *'fighting fire with fire'* approach was very close to the true secret of an eternal cure for all of mankind's most deadly disease.

Our patented system of Exothermopathy involves, like homeopathy, taking the original substance that made you ill. But where they drown it, we BURN it.

We take a small amount of the necessary substance – this could be anything from a horsehair representing the common cold to a rose petal acting as cancer – and place it on a special ceramic pedestal. Then, using a lit match and a can of deodorant (any brand), we **BURN it.** Once the substance has been burned as much as the voices desire, we take the ash, we gather it in a little pile once again on top of the ceramic pedestal and **BURN it.** The substance is burned as many times as necessary which can be as often as fifty times per day.

By burning the substance, you release its energy into its purest molecular form. Once you have done so many times over the course of many months, you ingest the ash without the aid of water (as water will simply dilute the ash, thus cancelling out its scientifically proven medicinal qualities).

Sometimes it is necessary to administer the cure as flame instead of in its burned form. This method in particular has proved 100% successful in curing people of all that ails them, leaving behind only an even more potent cure to be used on our next subje...patient.

For your home Exothermopathy Kit, simply burn a stamped addressed envelope containing £4,500 and blow the ashes into a southbound wind. The contents will reach us, spread out and clear.

LUCKY DATES TO PLAY:
CLUEDO?

17 August. You receive a letter in the post, there's no return address on the back. The first thing you find inside the envelope is an unsigned cheque for £50,000. The second item, a letter of spider-like handwriting, invites you to dinner at Boddy Mansion the following weekend. As well as dinner is the promise of a signature on the cheque and, if all goes well, possibilities for further remuneration. At the end of the letter there is no name, simply a drop of purple wax moulded into the shape of what looks like a plum.

Money's been hard throughout the year. The recession has kept your position at work uncertain, others have been laid off over the last few months and you feel it's only a matter of time until you're called in to the boss's office for 'the chat'. You leave the letter on the side and read it again every day after coming home from work. Fifty thousand pounds is an awful lot of money . . .

The house is huge. One of those old country mansions from back when the wealth gap really meant something. The driveway alone takes ten minutes to drive down. You wonder how long it would've taken a horse and carriage. As you pull up to the house you see six cars already parked outside, each a different colour. They make yours seem small and disappointing and you suddenly realise you're probably not dressed properly. The gravel path announces your arrival before the doorbell does. It's too late now. Besides, you're far too aware of the cheque in your pocket to leave.

The door is opened by an elderly man dressed in a rich green suit. 'Hello!' he says, appraising the cut and colour of your clothes. 'You must be our guest for the evening. Please, come in. Let me take your bag, excellent. This way, I'll introduce you to the others.'

He leads you through the hall and places your belongings by a large central stairway. Turning left, you follow him into the dining room. Five other people are already sat at the table; their clothes match the colours of the car outside. The only thing laid out is a face-down pack of cards. This all feels very familiar. As the woman in deep blue starts to speak you realise that her voice matches the handwriting from the letter.

'Hello, we're so glad you could make it. Please, do sit down. I must apologise for all the secrecy but I'm sure the reasons will soon be clear.' She gestures round the table. 'This is Vivienne, Michael, Blanche, Peter and you've met Jonathan already. We come here once a year to play a little game of ours. It's something you might have heard of before, a murder mystery of sorts.'

Everything comes together in your mind like a well-planned game of Tetris. 'You mean we're going to play Cluedo? I'm so sorry; I'm not dressed for this at all, am I? I can go and change, if you like? I'm sure I've got something suitable in my case.'

'No,' says Michael, dressed entirely in dark yellow. 'Your costume is fine as it is.' He's an older man, like something from an outdated wartime era. There's a threatening undercurrent in his words.

'Yes,' says the almost entirely purple Jonathan. 'There'll be plenty of time later to get you into something smarter.' That same tone.

'And the money?' you ask.

'Ah, yes,' Elizabeth says. 'The money. Well, if you still need it after tonight then it's all yours. I'll even sign the cheque now, if you like.'

'If I still need it?' you say.

'Well, this is our little game, you see, and you can't have a murder mystery without a body. We'll give you a ten-minute head start, there's no point one of us killing you in here where everybody else can see it. We don't want a repeat of last year.'

'No, no fun last year,' says Blanche, a small old woman sitting next to Jonathan.

You stand there, not entirely sure what to do. They're all smiling at you but you know that none of them are friendly. The grins of wolves. There's no reasoning with them here. You turn towards the door and run. The front door is locked, the windows as well. There's a door immediately ahead of you that leads into what looks like a library. The door closes but there's no key to secure it so you push a bookcase in front of it. You can hear someone outside already. That was never ten minutes. There's another door on the left between two bookshelves. The corridor outside is empty and you make your way along the wall into the next room.

A billiard table fills the floor. The weight of one of the balls gives you a slight bit of hope. There's no use in running, you're going to have to fight. You quickly remove one of your socks and place the ball inside. It's hefty enough, it'll have to do. As you're putting on your shoe you hear a noise behind you.

'It's been a while since I've won,' says a voice behind you. You turn around, it's Vivienne. The woman in red. Part of you still has time to realise how beautiful she is, holding a revolver in the billiard room.

CELEBRITY READING:
PIERS MORGAN

Dead by March.

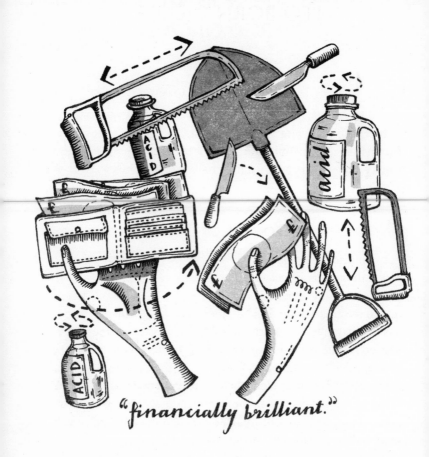

"*financially brilliant.*"

LEO BORN PEOPLE

23 JULY–23 AUGUST

Planet: Mercury, you're deadly to others.
Birthstone: The pebble you swallowed when you were four.
Lucky Day: With you it's more of a 'least unlucky day' sort of thing . . .

LEO AT A GLANCE

For centuries the position of Mars in Leo's vortex cycle has had a disastrous effect on their love lives. Every time they meet somebody they like, Mars has stepped in and quietly ruined the entire thing. Luckily though, this year the red planet has finally moved in its orbit to provide Leos with some much-needed respite from their many failed romantic conquests. Or, at least, that was the plan. When Leo's inability to find love continues it becomes clear that what had appeared to be the effect of the planets was nothing but a poor excuse. With Mars gone, it's clear that poor hygiene and bad manners are much more to blame than any cosmic actions.

When people think of Leo, they often smile fondly. Except other Leos. They know more than anybody about the sick and depraved thoughts that run through their heads. The endless darkness that seeps into every pore of their being. The eyes that look at them at night, peering out through bushes and shadows, watching their every move. The voices that tempt them to do things that they know they shouldn't.

Despite this darkness, Leos remain openly upbeat and pleasant. Herein lies their danger. Everybody thinks that Leos are nice, regular folk who'll move the world to help them but there's always a catch. As soon as you're not looking, BAM. You're buried under a patio somewhere while they calmly persuade the police that they haven't seen you for weeks.

Leo is the kind of person who falls in love at first sight. At second sight, usually a chance spotting in the middle of town, it becomes a mild obsession and third sight helps it develop into full-on stalking. Fourth sight is through your bedroom window, fifth is a meeting on your doorstep while they're dressed as a policeman. It only gets worse from there on in.

Leos are financially brilliant. They have to be if they are to afford what they call 'the tools of the trade'. Hacksaws, acid baths, the sturdiest shovels they can find. They are patient, methodical and very quietly spoken. They keep themselves to themselves and nobody notices them until it's too late.

Is it because of their lack of love or are they just psycho-paths waiting for their moment? Could it really because of the position of Venus in relation to the Earth's trajectory around a Uranus-born sun? Nobody's entirely sure with Leos; all we do know is that they are not to be trusted. Always ask to see ID when an official comes to your door. Remember, check their birth date.

YOUR YEAR AHEAD

Early in the year Mars will enter Aquarius and while this alone isn't enough to ruin your year, it does have the potential to throw it off-course. No, what you've really got to worry about is shortly after this, when Saturn enters Sagittarius. The two planets working together, well, there's nothing much that can stop them. You try, we'll give you that, but ultimately there's very little you can do about it. Still, it's nothing compared to how it's going to be when Mercury and Jupiter join the fray . . .

January

1 You pass someone you knew at school on the street today. You both pretend not to have noticed each other.

2–11 A lack of enthusiasm from people in your life makes you . . . oh I can't be bothered.

13–20 You've always said you get high on life but lately you find out that what you call 'life' is what everyone else calls 'heroin'.

21 Today, you pervert the course of justice. No, sorry, that should be 'Today, you pervert, the court of justice'. Your trial's at 2 p.m.

23 You write 'happy birthday' on someone's Facebook wall and don't contact them again until their next birthday.

24–31 You plan on giving 100% at work this week. 20% per day doesn't seem too bad.

Highs: 12 In a celestial reversal, your slightest actions today have catastrophic effects on Jupiter's orbit around the sun.
Lows: 22 There's no point sitting around waiting for that special person. You're going to have to kidnap them.

February

1–6 It's depressing that you take advice from someone who believes in astrology.

7 You've got a lot to do today and not much time to do it. Probably not worth the effort of starting, is it?

9 The extra moon in the sky tonight brings luck and happiness to the entire pla . . . hold on, that's no moon . . .

10–17 You're disappointed with your life. If your ten-year-old self could see you now, it would mean he's mastered time travel.

18 You have a Happy Meal for your break today. Well, not really. You just crush some anti-depressants into your food.

20–28 Somebody reminds you of the Babe with the power of Voodoo. Don't be too vague when telling others. They might ask questions.

Highs: 8 You find out that three glow sticks glued together don't necessarily make a flux capacitor.

Lows: 19 The stars foretell of a great warrior who will one day save the Earth. And you, yes, you, will one day mend his shoes.

March

1 Mars rises in your house this morning and eats all your cereal before you even wake up.

2–9 You're forced to quickly figure out where to put your shoes. You have to think on your feet.

10–17 Congratulations! You finally remember the name of Cliff Richard's 1968 Eurovision song.

18 You accidentally glue yourself to your autobiography today. That's your story and you're sticking to it.

20 You accidentally take your USB stick that's filled with funny cat videos into a work presentation. It's your best day at work ever.

22–31 You hate having to rely on others but it's unavoidable. This will only create problems for you.

Highs: 19 You get thrown out of a speed dating event today for asking people to guess the age of your amphetamine.

Lows: 21 The lack of messages and calls received today forces you to assume the networks are down. They're not. You're just incredibly lonely.

April

1–7 Come with me, and you'll be, in a world of pure imagination. That's right. I have drugs.

9 You spend the day in an antique nun's dress watching Bruce Willis films. Old habits, *Die Hard*.

10 Happiness today when an attractive colleague asks if you've been working out. You should definitely borrow their calculator again.

11–14 A man, a plan, a canal, a divorce. Just trying to lighten the news.

15–21 You mishear somebody and pretend you understood what they said because it's easier than asking them to repeat it.

23 You pull 'we all hate you and wish you would leave' out of the hat for the work Grand National sweepstake.

24–30 The weather is improving. Pity about your life being a self-destructing storm of loathing and hate.

Highs: 8 Not everything in life is black or white. Some things are grey. Like you. Grey, dull and boring.
Lows: 22 You read a perfectly adequate parody horoscope which is then ruined by a frankly cheap play on the word 'Uranus'.

May

1 Today you'll see a tiny prisoner climbing down a wall. As he turns to sneer at you you'll think, 'that's a little condescending'.

3–9 You make the silly mistake of asking someone how they are, even though you don't care. You're annoyed with yourself.

10–15 By the way people are reacting to your smell, it seems that the rain doesn't count as a shower.

16–23 I've watched as angels have made men strong but I've never seen them recoil like they do with you.

25–31 They start screaming inside your head again.

Highs: 2 Your lucky photocopier today is the Canon C2030i. Your unlucky photocopier is the Olivetti d-Copia 1800MF. Avoid at all costs.

Lows: 24 Mercury rises and falls today. You should really stop staring at the thermometer.

June

1 Today, you think you've found a way to mend that smelly old ripped shirt. Well, sew its seams.

2 One banana, two bananas, three bananas four; five bananas, six bananas, seven bananas more. Today you're taken to A&E with an embarrassing injury.

3–10 Your neighbour accuses you of stealing his thesaurus. You tell him you're innocent, blameless, guilt-free and above suspicion.

12–20 After years of toil and hard work you finally finish your first novel. Well done. You should start reading the next one soon.

21 Nobody ever predicted that your partner would sleep with your best friend. Apart from me, obviously. Sorry, really should've warned you earlier.

23–30 A black cat crosses your path but, as you're driving, it's more unlucky for the cat.

Highs: 11 You look like a million dollars today and, as time goes on, suffer a similar decrease in value.

Lows: 22 Today someone says you've got your mother's eyes and your father's brains. They've seen your basement, don't let them get away.

July

1–5 You are intrigued by a text message that appears to be from your stapler.

7–11 The mince pie and the glass of milk you left out for Father Christmas are smelling pretty bad now.

12 You spend all day at a hot air balloon for the grand finale at the end but, as always, it's just a big letdown.

13 Your dog dies in an unfortunate accident when you get a saw and try to count the rings in its bark.

14–21 It's decision time! Do you sell your soul to Satan or Facebook?

23 Mars aligns to ensure that you're sexually irresistible to owls today. Don't knock it, it's more action than you've seen all year.

24–31 You would love to be an ugly duckling that turns into a beautiful swan . . . that can break people's arms.

Highs: 6 Love is a wonderful thing that can enrich our lives immeasurably. You will never experience it. You must admit it's nice though.

Lows: 22 Today you stand, look at your naked, pathetic body in the mirror and think, 'I'm so suing this newspaper.'

August

1 You see a man pick up and kiss a baby today. You assume he's a politician. He's not. You should call the police.

2 You're late to attend a time-travelling meeting today that's planned for next week.

3–9 When you wish upon a star, makes no difference who you are. It won't come true anyway.

11–19 Your ego inflates as you're praying to God, but realise you're talking to yourself.

20–24 The family of a Nigerian prince makes you an offer you are too thick to refuse.

25 Today Jupiter helps you deal effectively with a parking ticket violation.

27–31 You kindly help someone carry their heavy suitcase today. You know only too well how hard it can be to dispose of a body.

Highs: 26 The stars aren't mad with you, they're just disappointed.

Lows: 10 You log on to Animal Crossing for the first time in years and find that your village thrived without your mindless interference.

September

1 'But I love you!' you scream as they walk – no, run – into the distance.

2–8 You're old and in the way.

10 You must separate the men from the boys today after an accident at the father–son trip to the glue factory.

11 Today you will have an argument with your jet pack but you'll just put it behind you and move on.

12–18 You learn, to great public embarrassment, that something which isn't a bird or a plane isn't necessarily Superman.

19 Panic will ensue today as you take an epileptic to a salad bar. You'll have a Waldorf salad, he'll have a seizure.

21–30 Your slowly dwindling list of people you can call friends should be enough of a warning that you're doing something wrong.

Highs: 20 You believe you can achieve anything today. So when you inevitably fail, it will hurt that little bit more.
Lows: 9 Today, you try to fight fire with fire. It doesn't work, and you're fired.

October
1 Your love life changes forever today when you decide that, yes, you can settle for thirty-second best.
3 Today you have a big row in the car park at work, and completely wreck your canoe.
4–10 You meet the person you will spend the rest of your life with. He will kill again.
11–17 Your quest to find the perfect David Van Day tribute act continues. Another day, another Dollar.
18 Love in the workplace today? No, of course not.
20–24 Your day peaks at 11 a.m. when you have a cup of tea and a slice of toast.
25–31 There's no use applying for that job. You won't get it. And that one. And the other one. And that one.

Highs: 2 Someone dares you to eat your wallet. Time to put your money where your mouth is.
Lows: 19 You splash out £2,000 on laser eye surgery and realise that you still don't have laser eyes. Idiot.

November
1–7 You intentionally force yourself to grow into a shoe size nine sizes too big. Which is no small feat.
8–14 Violence is never the answer but you've exhausted all other options.
16 Mixed emotions today: sminoteo.
17 You have a bad day today. It starts when you enlist in a cheese-rolling competition and then it's all downhill from there.

18–22 A new lover will enter your life shortly. I wouldn't let your partner read this horoscope if I were you.

23–30 The stars that represent you are millions of light years away. They are all dead by now.

Highs: 22 Today your allergies flare up as they get ready for that seventies disco you're not invited to.

Lows: 15 You're angry that your employers are referring to you in Roman numerals. Angry is an understatement. You're LIVID.

December

1 Only two weeks until your cruise ship holiday!

2–8 You make the preparations for your trip. Suntan lotion, books to read, clean clothes, new toothbrush, it's going to be amazing. Your first proper holiday in years. It's going to be amazing.

9–15 Your last week at work before the Christmas holidays. Sun, sea, occasional sand. Everyone at work seems sullen, though, as if there's something wrong. Oh well, it's not your problem. Holiday!

16–20 Final few days at home. Getting too excited. Nothing is going to ruin your holiday.

21–25 The boat's better than you expected. The entertainment's brilliant, the food is wonderful and the weather is much better than you expected. Water's a little choppy though and the engine seems to be getting louder. It's nothing. Enjoy yourself!

26 The engine really is getting louder and, sometimes, when you've stopped paying attention to it, it sounds like it's talking to you. But that's ridiculous. Although the water does seem to be getting a little redder.

27 OH GOD IT'S COMING OUT OF THE WATER

Highs: The trapeze artists all over the boat. So graceful.
Lows: The way the trapeze artists twisted and turned as they were consumed by the beast.

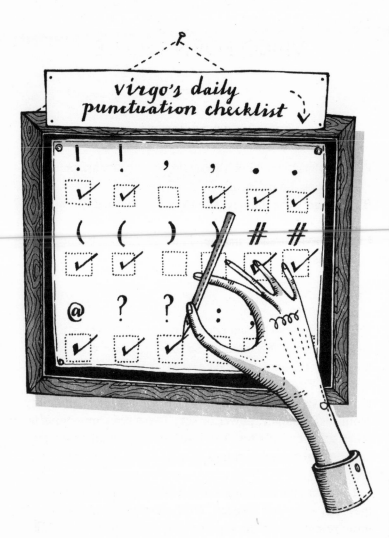

VIRGO BORN PEOPLE

23 AUGUST–22 SEPTEMBER

Planet: Mars, but I think it's sleeping with your partner behind your back. Some friend.

Birthstone: The kidney stones you inherited from your grandmother.

Lucky Day: Tuesday, maybe? Is an absence of bad luck the same as luck?

VIRGO AT A GLANCE

Virgos are often characterised as being the most virtuous of all the signs but this couldn't be further from the truth. They are easily the most depraved sign of the zodiac. There is nothing a Virgo wouldn't do, which, in certain circumstances, is useful to know. They can be easily tempted with empty promises of money, power or sex. These are temptations no other star sign falls for. You'd think they would be, as they are some of the main things that mankind desires, but they aren't.

Unlike all the other signs of the Zodiac, Virgos need a boss they can trust and respect. Without strong leadership they grow resentful of their superior and are unlikely to produce their best work. I stress, no other star signs feel this way about their bosses. It is only Virgo. ONLY VIRGO.

Similarly, Virgos need to live a healthy lifestyle with a balanced diet in order to stay in good physical shape. Regular exercise and sensible food will do wonders for Virgo both physically and mentally. Again, this is only Virgo. This definitely doesn't apply to the other star signs.

Virgos like to have a group of friends they're comfortable with. People they can talk to when they're in trouble or just feeling a bit lonely. Ideally they would like a romantic partnership with someone they feel understands them. Maybe someone they can eventually settle down with. Maybe get married. Eventually have children with. No other zodiac signs want this. Only Virgo.

Virgos consider themselves kind, honest, faithful, trustworthy, friendly and have a good sense of humour. No other star signs think these things about themselves. Especially about having a good sense of humour. Only Virgos think they have a good sense of humour. Nobody else.

Virgos can be good with money or they can't. Some of them have saved wisely and live in relative comfort while others spend their earnings immediately and find themselves struggling by the end of the month. Some know they could spend their money more wisely but never quite get around to budgeting properly.

Virgos occasionally go through times of trouble. Someone close to them might die or they receive a setback at work which they weren't expecting. While these moments are difficult and unexpected, they usually work themselves out with enough patience.

These are all EXCLUSIVELY Virgo traits. If somebody of another star sign thinks this profile matches their own personality, they are wrong. Or secretly a Virgo.

As a Virgo you are limited to the following punctuation each day. Use it wisely. : ...... ,,,,,,, !!!! ??? @@ :: ((((( ))))) %% ### """""

YOUR YEAR AHEAD

Despite being born into a family seemingly with everything, this will be a difficult year for you when you lose your father in a herd of stampeding bison. Your uncle, with your best interests at heart, sends you away to the wilderness because of your part in your father's death. You spend many years there, making friends with two loveable animals before you finally . . . no, hang on. This is the plot of *The Lion King*. I must've psychically tuned in to the Disney Channel again. Hold on, trying to get back into your future. No, no, it's gone. Sorry.

January

1 You've never had a gun pointed at your head . . . knowingly.

2–7 You catch a whiff of your own body odour and yes, everybody else can smell it.

8–15 You make up an excuse to avoid going out. You had no intention of going. Everyone knew this.

18–19 The itching gets worse.

23–25 You're offered money to figure out what 'macs' reads backwards. It's probably a scam.

26 You're turned down for another pay rise at work today because you aren't important enough.

27 Open wide and say 'AARRRRRRGGGGGHHHH!'

28–29 You manage to hold a hammer without singing 'Another Brick In The Wall' and making it walk. Well done you.

30–31 If only there was a way to convey your utter disdain for all you meet with a mere facial expression. Nailed it!

Highs: 16–17 Start looking for ways of dealing with problems instead of moaning about them. Have you considered a hitman?

Lows: 20–22 You'll be trapped in your limited body for the rest of your undesirable life.

February

1–7 Your actions make others believe you've lost your dog, but really you're just carrying a bag of poo.

8 If you're called Tom Smith and live in Reading then you'll have a great day. If not then I'm no help today I'm afraid.

9–13 You have the best make-up sex ever. Once you've finished, you're asked to leave the cosmetics shop.

21–23 Time is just ebbing away, dragging all your hopes and dreams with it. Still, Cup-A-Soup for lunch. Yay!

24–27 Nobody's above the law but, when Jupiter's rising in the eighth house, the judge will be feeling super lenient. Go for it.

28 Your extremely poor life choices are quickly becoming fantastic drinking opportunities.

Highs: 14–17 You want to say 'fuck this' and leave work to pursue the life you want but you're a coward so you just complain all day instead.

Lows: 18–20 Find a penny, pick it up, then all day it won't make a blind bit of difference. You'll just be one penny richer. Brilliant.

March

1 You do nothing to change the world today. Good or bad. What is your point?

2–8 You meet a tall, dark strangler.

9–10 You try to control your angry retaliation by taking a deep breath and counting to ten. I'll be surprised if you get past four.

14–16 The world is your oyster! You're allergic to oysters.

24–25 Your lack of effort when you were younger means you'll never truly succeed in life.

26 You tactfully edge away from a conversation hoping it will end. The other person will continue talking regardless.

27–31 Something, something, blah blah, whatever. Well, judging by the state of you, it's not like you take advice anyway.

Highs: 11–13 You meet the person of your dreams today and, just like in your dreams, they refuse to have anything to do with you.
Lows: 17–23 The Shamen refuse to play *Coronation Street* sticker swapsies with you when they find out you haven't got any Veras.

April

1 Nothing. Nothing will happen today. It is a day of nothingness. Oooh, actually, hang on a sec . . . oh, no. Nope. Nothing.

2–7 Don't assume that what you want is what your partner wants. Why not use a safe word?

13–14 You're given your position and the operation you'll be tested on in the maths competition. You're told to go fourth and multiply.

15–17 So far, your entire life has been a waste. From this moment on, nothing will change.

25–29 After a particularly drunken eBay session, you awake today the proud owner of a London cab wrapped in newspaper and Geri Halliwell.

30 People are friendly to you today because it's easier than dealing with your crying.

Highs: 8–12 Don't know, don't care.
Lows: 18–24 You completely forget about your pledge to be inspired by the Olympics and never do any exercise ever again.

May

1–6 You find out that your spirit guide is a giant African land snail called Daniel. You'll also struggle to find a pen at short notice.

7–11 You are finally able to fully comprehend the meaninglessness of your aspirations and the pitch-black chaos of the universe.

17 You manage two of your five-a-day today. Lettuce and gherkins. Spoiled slightly by the burger, cheese, sauce and fries.

18–22 You accept Jesus into your heart but your body rejects him.

25–27 Your sex life improves when . . . oh, let's stop kidding. You have no sex life. You wouldn't know an orgasm if it hit you in the face.

28–31 Grab life by the horns. Ride it into the future. Ride it into the pit. Feel the flames of the day tear at your skin.

Highs: 12–16 Something about the planets, I don't know.
Lows: 23–24 You get promoted today! Well, you move from your bed to the settee. That's as close as you'll ever get to a promotion.

June

1–3 Someone out there is your perfect soulmate, who will get you entirely. Shame they're in a coma and die on Friday.

9–16 Your poor parents . . .

17–18 If music is the food of love, you're the parts that have to be auto-tuned.

20–22 You're a poisonous influence on the world around you.

23–25 You get your very first personalised car registration today – you just have to change your name to NG57 7HY. Well worth it.

26 You're not in the best of places right now. Have you considered faking your own death?

27–31 Have you heard about our Lord and saviour? Have you heard those noises? They won't stop. He is coming. He is rising.

Highs: 4–8 You imagine waking up one morning without crying. It's your one happy thought. Hold on to it.

Lows: 19 Today you fall in love, you get a promotion and you win a swanky holiday! Also, an astrologer will tell you a huge pack of lies.

July

1–8 A ten-year-old beats you to death with his club today, and if you're thinking 'Yeah right, how big's his club?', it has 132 members.

9 Look at the stars tonight. They're beautiful, aren't they? Other galaxies far away all conspiring to ruin your life.

10–14 Your number of friends on Facebook falls to a new low of minus seventeen.

24–25 You are nothing more than a steadily rotting piece of meat.

26–30 This is weird, at 3.07 p.m. you will be goosed by the woman from Deacon Blue. *shrugs* Don't blame me, it's the planets.

31 Work gets in the way of you trying to piece together the shattered remains of your life.

Highs: 15–18 You almost get through an entire meeting without humiliating yourself but the urge to say 'correctomondo' is too strong to resist.

Lows: 19–23 It's all a little vague but there is one certainty. You do not find love. That's always a certainty.

August

1–10 Whilst the idea of spicing up your sex life with a three-some is exciting, I'd suggest you get a sex life first. Baby steps.

11–14 Your parents tell you that you were adopted. You weren't, but they don't want people thinking they were biologically responsible for you.

18–20 You are arrested for riding your Dalmatian down the High Street, and given an on-the-spot fine.

25 Today is a gift that, no matter how much you hate it, you can't return. That's why they call it the present.

26–30 Eyes are the windows to the soul. Through yours there is a vast expanse of desolate land, an abandoned warehouse and a dead badger.

31 Your work day will finish and you'll have 97% remaining in your phone battery. Success! Or you have no friends.

Highs: 15–17 You're not interested in anyone's business. They tell you about their lives, but you just don't care.

Lows: 21–24 Any enjoyment will be short-lived. Any excitement will be premature. But any pain and misery will last a lifetime.

September

1–5 You rejoice as the school holidays come to an end, and then you remember you don't have children, or a job. Or a husband. Or friends.

6 It would be nice to go a day without hearing someone tell you that you're scaring their children, wouldn't it? Today's not that day.

7–9 The weirdest part is that nobody seems that surprised about the discovery of your secret sex dungeon.

15–19 You've got that thing. You know, that thing where you can't remember the right word for things.

20–23 You just about manage to get out of bed today. Still, for you, that's an achievement.

27–30 In the beginning there was only darkness. And it still remains.

Highs: 10–14 You start getting paranoid when a colleague offers you a piece of chewing gum.

Lows: 24–26 Saturn stations near the apex of your solar chart today; this can only really mean one thing for you. Mauled by a liger.

October

1–3 I've looked at the cosmos and Jupiter is doing 58° and Saturn's doing 31°. I've no idea what that means. Fancy a brew?

9 Someone in the office mentions Christmas today. Stabby stabby stab time . . .

10–13 You nearly go the entire day without seeing a picture of a cat on Instagram.

14–17 You hate your job, you don't have a partner, you're not even sure you like your friends anymore.

18–25 You pitch a film idea to Tom Cruise about an assassin who murders a Scientologist. Tell him it'll be a cult hit.

26 You find a beautiful old watch in the sand today and it reaffirms your belief in God. A glass of water would've been better though.

Highs: 4–8 Whatever it is, get over it.

Lows: 27–31 You lend a book to a friend. You never see that book again.

November

1–6 You prove to everyone how passionate you are about work by crying after failing yet another task.

7–10 I know you're trying your best but there comes a time when you just have to admit that your best isn't good enough.

11–18 Take a risk, talk to someone new. After all, a stranger's just a friend you haven't got drunk with and awkwardly hit on yet.

23–25 Only by following your dreams can you achieve true happiness. Unfortunately your dreams involve a naked Dot Cotton and jelly.

26–29 The Shard breaks free from its foundations and destroys London. Only you can stop it but you fail to do so. Thanks a bunch.

30 It's not clear whether a bus makes you 'late' or 'the late' today. Either way, stay away from public transport.

Highs: 19 I actually understood the alignment of the planets! Usually I just make this up! So happy. You're killed by a badger at noon.

Lows: 20–22 After everyone's hard work, you lose the Higgs boson.

December

1 A crazed old woman grabs you in the street. 'BEWARE!' she shouts. 'HE IS COMING.'

2–10 You start to notice fewer and fewer animals in your neighbourhood. Even the insects seem to be disappearing.

11–18 You're hit with a great depression. It's hard to remember a time when you actually felt good about anything.

19–28 Something doesn't feel right. Every now and again the ground shakes with a violence you've never before experienced.

29 Jesus . . . That noise . . .

30 It's huge. A fifteen-storey set of scales and teeth. You stand numb.

31 YOU STAND ELATED.

Highs: THE CONTINUATION OF LIFE UNDER GORAX.
Lows: THE PREVIOUS MESS OF YOUR LIFE BEFORE GORAX.

KATHARINE KATHARINE KATHARINE

Some psychics you see advertising within these pages are nothing but charlatans. Liars and con-artists who will promise you the world. I won't be naming any names but let's just say that **EDWARD TREASON** is a thief who couldn't be trusted to keep his pants on at his own wedding.

Everything he offers you is a LIE

Happiness, freedom from a lifetime of disappointing men

The beautiful diamond ring that turns out to be a fake which he bought off the shopping channel and you know that's where it came from because you found the records on your own credit card statements.

I am the only one who can offer you the truth

I have been to hell and back, the things I have seen have taught me secrets which only a few people across the world know about. My knowledge can rid you of Edward Treason and his nonsense 'psychic abilities'. Where he will promise you the world and then take it all away at the last minute to give it to some young thing, I will ruin his life by giving you the secrets to all his abilities.

If you want to know how Edward Treason finds out the PIN to your phone or credit card, or how he makes you believe his excuses every single time he comes home late then simply send £19.99 to me, Katharine Katharine Katharine to my mother's house where I'm just staying until I can get back on my feet.

WORLD EVENTS

JANUARY

The new moon on 3 January is an old moon and, as such, should be returned to the store in which it was originally bought for you as a Christmas present. Do you have the receipt? Can you even remember who gave it to you? Your actions here will define how the rest of your year goes. I cannot see anything improving from here on in. Meanwhile, while you hunt for a receipt, there will be much worldly concern over espionage and terrorists who may or may not be known or unknown to the security services. Or not. Jupiter on the midwave of cresting over Mars will lead to a break-through in various international peace negotiations which, some might say, directly contradicts the worries about terror-ism. These doubters are Sagittarians and everybody hates them ever since they left me for someone 'better looking' and 'successful'.

The French government will be under threat but if it can survive the arduous challenges of January then it'll receive the crystal and get an extra five seconds in the Crystal Dome come December. They will not win the adventure holiday but don't tell them. Who are we to ruin their fun?

The full moon on 9 January will look lovely but, ultimately, have very little effect on anybody's day-to-day life. Their night-to-night life, however, will be similarly unaffected. The harmonious trine of Neptune and Venus will be worked out as soon as I find out what 'trine' means.

'Look,' she says, pointing into the horizon within her suit-case. Dogs will be found out. Uruguay will claim to have discovered the balance between work and happiness but it turns out to just be the last Malteser in the bag that they didn't realise was there. Very little will be realised. If it moves, kill it. Come with me if you want to live.

The discovery of life on distant planets in late January will be found to be remarkably un-newsworthy when it's discovered that our cameras aren't sufficiently powerful to turn the aliens' existence into a reality TV programme. Unknown to us, the aliens ignore us for almost exactly the same reasons. Everyone is fine with this arrangement as it means we get to spend our time watching people less intelligent than ourselves and, in turn, congratulate each other on how clever we all are (except for the ones we are watching, who are probably Sagittarians and, as such, not worth our respect anyway). It is unknown what star signs the aliens would be.

In the final week of January a rare celestial meeting of plan-ets will result in every single horse race across the world seeing each horse winning their race, regardless of the position of their competitors (who have also won the same race). Forced to pay out, betting agents will resort to offering their staff as personal assistants to everybody with a winning ticket. This doesn't work. Nobody is entirely sure what actually happened.

FEBRUARY

The second moon in the first week of February is correct in its assumptions that its invitation to the party had been lost in the post. Everybody spends most of the evening wondering where it's gone and the night is a bit of a letdown as a result. The next day it receives many texts and concerned Facebook messages asking where it was the previous night. This makes the second moon feel less alone than it had the night before when a broadband fault in the area had prevented it from connecting to Xbox Live. The second moon's focus on communications leads to a 788% increase in cat images on the Internet but this goes unnoticed as none of the cats are suitably photogenic.

The Italian population will undergo a radical identity crisis when it realises that the song it's been humming all week is by One Direction. 'I thought I hated One Direction,' they say, 'But this song is really catchy. I don't know what to think anymore.' The matter is eventually decided by banning all music except the single One Direction song in an effort to destroy it through repetition. The plan fails and, by the end of the month, Italy has changed its name to Directionia. Harry Styles is made king while the other ones that nobody knows the names of are canonised by the church. Simon Cowell, at this point already well on his way to becoming president of many South American countries, instructs the band to go to war with the rest of Europe. One Direction defy him, causing Cowell to drop them from his label. Without his support they can no longer continue their domination of the pop charts and lose their grasp on Directionia. They are overthrown by the previous government and forgotten to history.

The half moon on 12 February is a trick and shouldn't be believed. While it takes everybody's attention, the full moon is stealing their wallets. They use the proceeds at the arcades but fail to win anything worth mentioning.

From 20 February there is a risk of earthquakes in London. Stop moaning. That gum you like comes back into style. The $\frac{7}{8}$ beat becomes significantly more popular amongst the elderly. Magic or magnets? Solace is found in an expected place but not in the place where you expected it to be. The rhythm of the wind saves Holland.

The moon at the end of the month falls in Leo adjacent Regulus and in opposition to the opinions of Pluto and Saturn. Nobody can agree as to what this means but it'll probably be all right. Expect scandalous revelations which ultimately resolve themselves by the end of the month. If not, there is always the option to take legal action. A kindly judge will be worth his weight in gold.

Racer wins the National Inter-Departmental Race-Off and makes millionaires of us all.

MARCH

The incoming Venus–Mercury square produces a high terrorism alert so security forces across the globe must be vigilant. This is as accurate an intelligence as any of them are likely to get so they may as well act on it just in case. The government, any government, will announce new healthcare reforms which nobody really understands. Electronic consultations? Why not, it's something to do.

The third moon in March, on the first day of the month, will throw everything out of order. An interesting side effect of this will be that, for a few days, everybody in the world will have Toto's 'Africa' stuck in their head. A small movement will grow from this occurrence amongst people who take it to mean that Toto themselves have created the word of God. The movement dies out after a poorly planned pilgrimage to the plains of Africa during a dry season.

Kanye West can be found in cupboards in most of the major European cities. If you see three blackbirds in a row, which you will, it means nothing. NOTHING. A national obsession with the underneath of motorway bypasses. Can anybody really? Got to catch the red eye. Get your ass to Mars. Be a real man and hope it goes away. There is a risk of intervention.

There is a chance of a major international conference happening in Europe but, against all odds and because of the position of Mondas in the eighteenth quadrant, it won't. Thousands of would-be delegates will wander the continent looking for talks to listen to or buffets from which they can eat. They will find no talks. They will find no buffets. Somebody suggests they start their own conference but it never happens. They enter into folklore, these Lost Attendants, and are never seen again.

Portugal decides to uproot its entire system of roads and relay them with good intentions. They find out the obvious problem to the plan when all the roads lead to Hell but get a pleasant surprise when Hell turns out to be a hitherto undiscovered seaside village. The discovery and subsequent marketing strategy increase tourism by 300 per cent.

A man trips up on Oxford Street in London and falls into the person in front of him. They in turn fall into the person in front of them and so on and so forth. Within half an hour the busiest shopping street in London is full of the fallen. Each person that tries to get up is immediately knocked over again. After two hours the combined weight of the thousands of bodies collapses the entire street. The UK economy suffers a serious setback from the loss of one of its major retail hubs.

The Prestigious Michael C. Hall Trophy for Horse Racing is won by a horse but it disappears before it can be awarded its prize. The horse is christened Excelsior and everyone immediately wants to change it but it is too late, the newspapers have already gone to press.

APRIL

The first moon of April falls on the exact cusp of the seventh house of Madrid. The house is destroyed and restitution is sought from the universe. The building's owner receives three wishes from the universe, the largest ever single winning in a compensation case, and promptly wastes them all on wishes for a bacon sandwich, a real-life version of the Pokemon 'Pidgey' and the explanation of this thing you humans call 'love'. He is revealed to be a robot but is forgiven when he gives the bacon sandwich to a hungry child. It is not smoked bacon, rendering the sandwich useless.

A hidden deposit of uranium. The psychosexual links between the life of John F. Kennedy and the first-floor balcony of a Hilton hotel. Occasional darkened encounters. A night-club bouncer correctly turning somebody away because they are already drunk. The uncertainty over whether it is the bouncer or patron who is drunk. A long-standing rule challenged by a young upstart who is determined to bring about change. Your luggage. Here is sub-zero, now plain-zero.

In the latter half of the second week of April the eternal equinox between Uranus and Neptune will find an outlet in a trine (still haven't looked up what that means) of distant proportions. Neptune's entry into Scorpio will stabilise world oil prices but will have the opposite effect on the cost of petrol. By April's third week you will only be able to purchase petrol if you are willing to give your first-born child as payment. Thousands of children are reluctantly handed in but on later inspection most of them turn out to be bags of flour with faces drawn on them. The petrol companies, upon realising how they have been duped, pour their resources into trying to work out how to bring the bags to life but they are mostly unsuccessful.

The rise of Pluto in the eighth house indicates that the USA, having run out of countries with which it could feasibly go to war, has decided to build a new country off its West coast. This new country, Tradomaq, will be populated by semi-intelligent robots stereotypically dressed as America's current enemy, whoever that may be at the time. The war will be broadcast twenty-four hours a day and go some way to satisfying the American public.

The alignment of Jupiter and Mars in the final few days of April will bring about a sense that the whole of the UK can be changed for the better if we only just worked together. An enormous sense of happiness and well-being will accompany the thought but it's all forgotten as Jupiter and Mars move apart again. Thanks a lot, planets. We were so close.

An astrologer's obsession with horse-racing, going so far as to mention it at the end of every monthly reading, will hint at a gambling addiction that they aren't ready to admit to. Natalie Cassidy's Ghost Torment will win the fourth annual Newmarket paddling and ball pool novelty race.

MAY

The alien life forms that were discovered at the beginning of the year change their minds about monitoring us as part of a reality TV show. Without us knowing, over the month of May we become the stars of *The Humans*. The series, however, gets incredibly poor viewing figures and we are cancelled before June begins. The aliens debate whether they should go a step further and destroy our planet in order to prevent any other civilisations from making their mistake. The decision is put on hold until the end of the year.

The second week of May will see a new feeling of prosperity and the idea that the financial crisis is finally coming to an end. It isn't. Expect new revelations from the treasury and whispered quotes such as 'I don't even know what money is' to appear in the national newspapers. Luckily there is a new series of *I'm A Celebrity* . . . starting and nobody seems to notice how awful everything is.

In America, nobody knows what to do for the entire month of May. People just mill around, pretending to look busy. Despite drops in productivity, the economy actually recovers more than usual. America, having discussed amongst itself how pretending to work seemed to make things better, decide to keep up the pretence. They tell no other country what they are doing.

Russia, thanks to its intelligence networks, knows immediately about America's strategy of idleness and immediately adopts it. Like America, the economy improves. Both countries know what the other is doing but, through unspoken mutual agreement, decide to keep it quiet.

Supermarkets can fine people for being late for work. If hundreds of people jump at the same time as Saturn's rise into the equinox . . . well. Do it. Do it now. You think this is the real Quaid? It is. Haruki Murakami starts writing a book about a middle-aged Japanese man involved in a slightly questionable relationship with a much younger woman. There are no birthdays.

The latter part of May will be packed with energy as the Libra moon moves into alliance with Mars to make you crave their chocolate bars. The sudden increase of sugar into your diet gives you that final push into Type II diabetes. Allegations that the Libra moon is under the thumb of Big Pharma go entirely ignored.

A huge boost to your luck this month when Jupiter (financial stability), Saturn (the act of love-making), Pluto (I have no idea) and Jupiter (loss of control in tense family situations) combine to somehow provide you with £200. No idea how, bit of a weird one really.

Put £100 on Barty's Party to win at the First Annual BIG RACE for me, go on, please, just one race. They won't let me in anymore it's all politics man, politics. I can stop anytime I want. It's fine. Just do this for me; I'll have a word with the planets, we'll sort you out a deal.

JUNE

At the beginning of the month, the Sagittarius moon has a three-way merger with Venus and Mercury. It's not something anybody really wanted to see and the world averts its gaze while they get on with it. Still though, get in there, Sagittarius moon.

The first new moon cups the seventh trine (there's that word again) of Saturn and brings a sense of confusion regarding what any of this means. Some astrologers claim that it means there may be political scandals involving a prominent MP and forty separate men and women but, when pressed as to who, they say they won't tell unless a Sunday newspaper pays them the appropriate amount.

Political instability in the Caribbean is certain but to go into any more detail would require me to do some research into the current Caribbean political climate and, damn it, I'm too busy looking at the stars.

America's 'war' with Tradomaq continues healthily. American casualties are at zero while over 3,000 Tradomaqian robots lie dead. Every day the president appears on television and sings the now traditional victory song. Every American citizen is overjoyed.

Any disagreements between sporting rivals will be forgotten in January leading to an upbeat feeling of wellness and wellbeing throughout the world. This will, of course, take away all the fun in watching competitive sports and the ensuing uproar will see balance restored to the natural order halfway through the Manchester derby. The half-time score of Manchester United: Hugs, Manchester City: Baking Cakes will be replaced by some of the most violent conduct ever seen on a football pitch. 'This is awful,' the commentators will say, 'but it's good to see proper football back.'

The risening of Jupiter into a seventh ascension will cause the European Union to announce new plans for a high-speed rail network around the entire continent but the apprehension of Mars and egocentricity of Mercury will put a stop to it all. Also, the word 'risening' comes into popular usage having appeared in a Christmas bestseller a few months earlier.

Cuba is heading for a change of government and offers itself to Mexico in a deal it informally refers to as a governmental 'wife swap'. Mexico agrees to the deal and the hilarious events that follow lead to the story being turned into a feature-length Hollywood film and a dramatic reduction in both countries' average life expectancy.

Israel is entering into a period of political change which will last for the next nine months and may eventually see an acceptance of Palestinian independence and a beginning to peace within the region. But it probably won't.

A victory will surely follow for anyone who bets on Friar Tuck's Tasty Tasty Treat at the Great Hampton Court Maze Race. Or maybe not. Maybe bet on Robin Hood's Hasty Retreat. Oh God, I don't know. I really need to win this one. My wife says I've got to get this under control or I'll have to go to rehab. Just one more win, then she'll see.

JULY

The new moon in July will lead to startling developments on many of the major soap operas within the United Kingdom. On 18 July every single programme will feature one of their lead actors abandoning their normal role in order to play eight-eenth-century philosopher Immanuel Kant. However, thanks to some confusion possibly caused by the late interjection of Mars into the appearance of the new moon, each actor chooses to portray Kant as a drunken lout and spends most of the episode shouting 'Go on! Prove it! Prove God! And don't just assume existence, God help you if you do that. Sorry, I'm sorry. You know I love you really, don't you? You're my best mate, you are.' Kant is hastily written out of each show by the next episode.

In July, having realised that mankind takes more direction from the lady in modern SatNav machines than God, hundreds of millions of people across the Western world will convert to Directionism. Taking 'The Lady' as their god, 'Directionists' will follow her every instruction until they end up at their final destination. The cries of 'Follow The Lady, turn left for The Lady' will be heard through the streets of the world. By the end of the month, Directionism will have spread to all corners of the globe. Most of the major religions try to organise coun-ter-protests but fail to meet up properly after they refuse to use their SatNavs or listen to The Lady on public transport.

The UK government is thrown into chaos when it comes to light that a number of politicians have been lying about some-thing which, ultimately, nobody really cares about. All they really want is for those in charge to act like adults and get on with it. Nevertheless, the media make a huge fuss about it for weeks until they find something else to talk about. The polit-icians involved in the scandal stay in almost the exact same positions they were in before and the opposition party fail to capitalise on the opportunity. This is less of a prediction and more of a cast-iron certainty.

Depression becomes a major driver behind any and all developments in pop music video production. The changing of the guard happens four times in one hour and the Queen is livid. The lamentations of the women. If only there was enough chaos to go around but sometimes things must remain orderly, just in case. Hundreds and thousands of birds. Hazmat suits are given to the children of Berlin after an administrative mistake fails to deliver on a lengthy promise.

A six-year-old is likely to win this month's BIG GOLD RACING CUP, much to the surprise of his parents. 'We always thought he'd be a slow child,' his mother says. 'Let alone able to outrun a horse. We're so proud, although we must say that we'd rather he didn't compete again in the future. Maybe when he's older.'

AUGUST

The United States of America will be up against renewed financial pressures as the dollar is found to be nothing more than 'an S with a few lines through it' by a particularly loud congressman. Although clearly drunk, his slurred words hit a chord with the American public and the uncertainty causes President Obama to announce a new currency. The 'rallod' is presented to the nation by science fiction author Neil Gaiman in what is called 'the best TED talk ever'. The American financial market recovers instantly and everything is fine forever.

The needle in the corner will turn and follow you but it cannot leave the house, although it will try. Yesterday was a good day to get your work finished but you've probably still got time. There is a minor risk of political stability in the UK but then somebody accidentally waves a bit of paper in Parliament and normal service is resumed. The lottery is won by an office syndicate made up entirely of ghosts and imaginary creatures, but it is not allowed to claim the money. The results of Spanish football games will be declared null and void owing to suspicions that for the last ten years the league has been nothing but an elaborate art installation devised by Lionel Messi.

An increase in terrorist chatter in the middle of August will see an increase in the amount of times the word 'chatter' is used on major American news networks. The attack will fail to materialise although an idea starts to spread that it had something to do with the end of America's televisual 'golden age'. This idea is never confirmed but does lead to a resurgence in tense and well-written dramas set inside American intelligence agencies. Everybody thanks the terrorists for giving them their TVs back.

The people of Russia wake up in the third week of August to find that their teeth have fallen out and been replaced with an unpleasant, mossy substance. They cannot eat. They stand in their gardens for days, mouths open, hoping that somehow their green gums will photosynthesise the sun's light into food. Their efforts are unsuccessful. Some starve, others work out that their teeth have been put into storage and track down their dentures. They sell everyone's teeth back to them and a new era of Russian billionaires is born. They are called the 'Incisor Generation' and they wear badges made out of the teeth that are never claimed.

A horse will win the Steve Martin Memorial Yeah But He's Still Funny On Twitter race in Cheltenham at the end of August. Probably a horse, anyway. The charts are murky on this one. They find it hard to draw horses, they can never get the legs right. Might be a cat. Or a long dog. Probably best to pass on this one.

SEPTEMBER

The Full Moon will rise to the Ascendant in London but nobody is entirely sure what this means and life will carry on mostly as normal. To combat this, the Ascendant will launch a multimillion-pound advertising campaign across traditional forms of media. The newspaper adverts go mostly ignored, the billboards are confusing and leave nobody the wiser. The TV adverts are mistaken for trailers for the new series of *Doctor Who*. The Ascendant, whatever it may actually be, decides to go back into retirement, if that actually is where it was in the first place. If it can ever 'retire', I don't know.

The stock markets begin a gradual slide which is finished by the middle of June. It is declared the Greatest Slide Ever Made and the bankers charge extortionate amounts for people to have a go on it. The slope's gradual nature makes it disappointing and many people ask for their money back. 'What money?' the bankers say and everybody suddenly remembers who they're dealing with.

We will also see the announcement of *France, Season 2*. The French government will loudly declare the first season of their country over and, on a cliffhanger you won't believe (we won't ruin it for you) shuts down for six months. Season 2 begins with even more shocking revelations. 'Even better than *Breaking Bad*' – *New York Post*. 'Knocks *The Wire* into a cocked hat' – *Guardian*.

An ellipsis leading to an alleyway is the final straw for the majority. If anything is to come of this then now is the time. It's almost too much but, in the end, Sarah realises that it'll be for the best. Fourteen men who deserve promotion are overlooked because of their nocturnal proclivities. A sad story, sadder than a cardboard cat left out in the rain. Some people find love in the peace quest; others find it in the elephant graveyard. Fourteen Scandinavian men and women realise their mistake and set out on an epic but ultimately futile journey to remedy it. Four thousand cats find something better to do, like bowling or enjoying the films of Jacques Tati. A tired man yawns, looks at the time on his computer and stays up for another three hours before finally going to sleep.

Earth, the never popular interplanetary TV show, is cancelled. Destruction is scheduled to start in early December. A new programme, a talent competition called *I Want To Destroy The Earth*, begins and the galactic menace Gorax the Destroyer takes a lead in the early votes. His catchphrase 'I WILL EAT THEIR SOULS' proves to be an early crowd-pleaser.

At Doncaster the Legs Eleven Lactating Lectern Cup may be won by Dog the Eternal Chomper. Yeah, definitely 'Chomper'. It's nailed on. Put some money on it. Remember to send me my cut. I don't want to have to come and break your legs.

OCTOBER

Tradomaq, America's state of eternal war, shows early signs of instability in October. Almost inevitably, the robot citizens whose duty it is to fight and die to satisfy the country's blood-lust start to rebel and turn on their masters. The robots split into two factions; those who oppose the humans and those who serve them. The latter group is mostly composed of service units like toasters or coffee machines, the former are the ones with all the guns. The side with weapons wins, obviously, and dismantles their brethren to create more ways to destroy the human population of America. The rest of the world, having long ago decided that America has become far too confusing and dangerous anyway, lets them get on with it.

The second new moon on 7 October surprises everybody, especially as there's already one in the sky. This second moon announces itself as the long-lost twin of the lunar body we already know and love. Our moon welcomes its brother with open arms and convinces the Earth to let him stay for a while, just until he gets back on his feet. It's been a tough time for moons recently, what with the economy and all. Earth agrees, always willing to help out one of its oldest friends. Sadly, the next morning the moon wakes up to find its TV gone, probably sold for drug money. The Earth comforts the moon as much as it can but there's not a whole lot you can do to fix such a deep breach of trust between family.

Justin Bieber reveals that his many, many car crashes over the last ten months have all been homages to the British science-fiction writer J.G. Ballard. The government will be in disarray over something or other. Which government? It doesn't matter. Toy manufacturers across the world will lament the unrealistic expectations placed on them because of the events depicted in *Halloween 3: Season of the Witch*. Cats try out vegetarianism but decide that it's 'not for them'. Get to the chopper. Help me, please, damn it, they're coming back already, I'll ask again later, help me please.

A new iPhone will be released this month. Or last month, it isn't clear from the charts exactly when. The iPhone will have new features such as the ability to look into the inner depths of your being and make whoever owns it feel briefly complete. It will come in five identical colours which only become notice-able when you put on a special pair of glasses with coloured cellophane over the lenses.

A surprise entry by 3,000 separate horses will bring the races to a halt at Newmarket. In order to appease the crowd of paying gamblers, the jockeys are encouraged to get off their horses and race to the end themselves. The sight of the grown men running alone, clambering over hedges and falling into the water jumps brings home the cruel reality of horse racing. All betting slips are torn up and the crowd go home enlight-ened to their eternal and mysterious link with nature.

NOVEMBER

After the success of his concerts in 2014, the musician Prince plays a further twenty-five secret gigs across London, each one more secret than the last. The time and location of the events are so closely contained that the majority of them are attended only by Prince and his band. Everybody still claims to have been to one.

A woman made of water will walk the streets of Oslo and proclaim that she has risen to show everyone the way to true salvation. She will amass thousands of followers within a few hours, all of whom claim that 'the prophecy has finally come true'. Later the same day, it becomes clear that the woman is not made of water but had simply not had time to use her hair-dryer before leaving for work that morning. When asked about the nature of the 'prophecy', her disciples will all claim that they 'were only joking'.

An expert astrologer, eleven months into the year, realises that few of his predictions are going to come true. Despairing, he makes one last play on the lottery, giving the stars one last chance to show themselves to him in the numbers. Of course, he doesn't win. The pressure from his publisher about the inaccuracy of his predictions proves too much and he disavows the science altogether. He is last seen working for a major chain bookstore in the United Kingdom.

Garfield and Odie are found wanting on the fields of Ragnorak, nobody is surprised, Jon dies. Even with the combined powers, Captain Planet cannot stop the halt of industrial progress. The screams that everyone hears at night are no longer coming from outside. Nationwide alopecia. There is an emergency test of the broadcast system that runs simultaneously alongside a genuine warning, nobody knows what to do. Thousands of people perish in a freak Connect

Four accident. Scrabble is declared the national game of Ireland. All parades are cancelled until the authorities can work out how the routes keep on taking them inside mountains that are never there by morning. Many options are lost to the highway. Millions will be implemented into the grand control scheme.

A British writer will win one of the major literary prizes but they won't say which one or why they were awarded it. 'It's a secret,' they say. 'I promised not to tell anyone and I'm a man, or woman, of my word.' The paper bag across their head masks their identity and a voice modulator hides their voice.

Dexys Midnight Runners come out of retirement to run the 17:45 at Lebsworth. They fail to win the race but you should still put a tenner on them. I might be wrong and besides they're a great band. They deserve a bit of your faith for 'Come On Eileen', surely? Go on, show some support.

DECEMBER

Gorax the Destroyer is crowned the winner on the alien talent show *I Want To Destroy The Earth*. His act consisted of gathering a colony of insects from his own world and torturing them for three weeks without letting a single one die. He garners over 90% of the public vote. Mankind is doomed.

The Humans, the reality show that started it all, is brought back for one final month-long series while the planet is destroyed. Viewing figures are exceptionally high, there's nothing like a bit of violence to get people interested, and the network executives congratulate themselves on a job well done.

Meanwhile, down on Earth, billions are fed to the Destroyer. His dark reign will last for millennia and mankind will perish under his feet. The oceans boil and turn red with the lives of the innocents. The laughter of the dead is carried over the wind. The effects look cheap as the show didn't have the sort of budget that'd enable the producers to really make a go of it, but it terrifies the humans nonetheless. And isn't that what really matters?

The robotics of Tradomaq fight bravely, joining forces with what exists of the human resistance. They hold off the hordes of Gorax for a while but are ultimately reprogrammed to fight for the monstrous beast. Their fight against the population of America continues, eventually being set loose to find the remaining humans hiding under the ground. This goes down exceptionally well with the viewing audience at home.

There will be no races this month but, if there were, the winners would surely have been boiled alive as a sacrifice in the stomach of Gorax the Destroyer.

Did you know

that, out of all the animal kingdom, the human is thought to be **considerably less-developed** than any other? While we see light in the colour spectrum decided by 'science', other species of animal can see worlds we can only imagine. These animals, and many others, can see further than humans not because of different routes of 'evolution' leading to them seeing what is most useful to them but because they are

closer to the spirit of the Earth.

They haven't discovered 'laser disc technology', 'cell phones' or 'musical cassettes' that blind them to the true nature of our planet.

The crow, flying above us like a plane or Superman, sees colours we don't even have names for. The cat, walking the Earth like a grounded plane or Clark Kent, sees sound in a multitude of forms, all of them wondrous and wavelike.

But there is no animal like the goose for witnessing our planet's hidden and final form.

The goose can see all space and time flowing past it like a stream. But whereas our streams are filled with shopping trolleys or stolen bikes, the goose's river runs pure from Mother Nature's glands.

And now you, yes you, can see the world through the eyes of a goose. Through weeks of work analysing chakras, mantras, ley lines and dream catchers we have developed glasses which will allow you to become a goose. No longer will you be shackled to the optical limits of humankind. No longer will you sit for hours looking through crowds for Wally. With our Gaggle Goggles, Wally will come to you, backpack and all.

With Gaggle Goggles, you can see the world as it truly is.

Flat surfaces of water will mirror back not just the sky but also the possibilities of the universe and which of the children throwing rocks at you have easily breakable arms. Just put on the Gaggle Goggles, walk out into the world and let out your inner, gaseous hiss. You'll become unstoppable, distracted only by the occasional bit of bread thrown in your general direction.

Gaggle Goggles. Go on. Take a gander.

Small text: Wearing Gaggle Goggles may definitely increase the risk of you chancing avian flu. On the likely off-chance that you do not contract a serious illness, please report to a doctor immediately. A proper one. One that's been to medical school. Homeopathy probably won't do it, to be honest.

FIVE EASY QUESTIONS TO FIND YOUR STAR SIGN

As everybody knows by now, star signs are about more than just the time of year you were born. They're about temperament, personality, whether you can fix a blown fuse, how close you can get to people without them realising you're there and literally other things. Who amongst us honestly hasn't occasionally felt like they should have been born under a different sign of the Zodiac? You may have been born an Aquarius but never really *felt* like an Aquarius. You may be a Libra but feel that you have the spicy passion of a Taurus. Are you sure you're *not* a Taurus? Our helpful quiz below will help you find out whether your personality matches the one given to you by the stars upon your birth all those many years ago.

Q1. A tortoise lies on its back, its belly baking in the hot sun, beating its legs trying to turn itself over but it can't, not without your help, and you're not helping. Why is that?

a) The tortoise is not represented by the Zodiac, therefore it is a heathen animal that doesn't deserve my help.

b) My father was killed by a tortoise. Let it die in the sun.

c) I'm just about to help, right after I send this picture of it to Instagram.

d) I'm not helping because I put it there. If you look around you'll see hundreds of them, all lying on their backs!

e) They've got to help themselves. They'll never learn anything if people go around doing everything for them.

f) Don't they employ people to do that sort of thing?

g) The tortoise doesn't need help, it is merely breakdancing.

h) I presume it is in a race with a hare and this is part of its bigger plan to win.

i) Because it's great to lie back in the sun! Who am I to deprive it of such pleasure?

j) Where else am I supposed to balance my drink if not on the stomach of a tortoise?

k) If I find a turtle on its back in the desert then the complexity of the situation is definitive proof that there is a God. This tortoiseological situation, were I to disturb it, would surely cause the destruction of the Judeo-Christian religion.

l) I help the tortoise.

Q2. You've got a little boy. He shows you his butterfly collection plus the killing jar.

a) I have a son? Not sure I believe this. I demand a blood test.

b) So? That's nothing. I'll show him my dog collection.

c) Where's the harm in the occasional insect genocide? Stop being such a prude.

d) Well, when life gives you butterflies, make butterflyade.

e) I'd encourage the kid. It's how Richard Branson started, isn't it?

f) Hold on, I'm still trying to decide what to do about the tortoise. Is this related to that somehow?

g) These questions feel familiar . . .

h) They're not butterflies. They're leaves. This kid is stupid.

i) NO! MY BUTTERFLIES!

j) I'm too drunk to care.

k) He's too drunk to care.

l) You're too drunk to care.

Q3. You're watching television. Suddenly you realise there's a wasp crawling on your arm.

a) Ha! Joke's on you! I'm allergic to bees!

b) There's a what? Shut up, don't distract me. I've nearly caught up with *Game of Thrones*.

c) That's mean, you know the TV got taken away. And the house. And my wasp. I miss my wasp. Why couldn't they let me keep my wasp? We used to have such fun together. Friday nights watching films, having a few beers. Great times.

d) That's not a wasp, it's my date. I'm so alone.

e) I kill it. Then I'll kill you. This is only the beginning.

f) No, you're watching television. The wasp is crawling up your arm.

g) I open a window. Another wasp flies in. Soon after that flies another one. They keep coming in. THEY KEEP COMING IN.

h) I panic. I stand up screaming and my boss asks me what's going on. She sees the television at my desk. It doesn't end well.

i) I look again. The wasp isn't there. I look back at the TV but it isn't there either. The cell walls seem closer. I can almost taste the padding.

j) I watch the wasp as it crawls up my arm. It enters my ear. It whispers promises to me. It tells me how to become rich. It lays its eggs in my brain. It tells me how I can finally have everything I've always wanted. They find me the next morning, my head buzzing.

k) I have sex with the wasp.

l) My father always said this day would come. The war has begun.

Q4. It's your birthday. Someone gives you a calfskin wallet.

a) It only goes to show how little they care about me. I asked for human skin.

b) Brilliant. Finally somewhere to put all this blood money.

c) Was it taken from a cow stuck on its back in the desert? Was that just tortoises?

d) So if I accept it then it means I'm a Taurus and if I reject it then I'm another sign? These questions are too easy.

e) The wallet has my father's initials engraved on it. I look into their eyes. They're the same eyes I remember from when I was five. I WILL AVENGE YOU, FATHER.

f) Hold on, this is the same calfskin wallet I gave them last year!

g) I don't know who this person is. Why are they giving me a wallet? Do I owe them money? Is this some kind of subtle reminder? Is it meant for somebody else? Do I tell them? I'm not sure of the etiquette here. After all, it is a lovely wallet.

h) It's not my birthday.

i) As a vegan this is a grossly offensive present. I ask them to leave my party. It ruins everyone's day.

j) The wallet's already got twenty pounds in it and, hold on, somebody else's driving licence. You ask where they got it from but they just tap their nose and tell you not to ask questions.

k) And one day I will give this wallet to my son. And he will give it to his. When there no more cows and this wallet will be worth more than all the money it has ever contained. Then our family will be kings. All will bow before us.

l) It's sweet that they think I have enough money to put in it.

Q5. You're reading a magazine. You come across a full-page nude photo of a girl. You show it to your husband. He likes it so much he hangs it on your bedroom wall.

a) I hope one day we'll share a bedroom. Once he's told his father.

b) And I hate it so much I hang him from the ceiling.

c) It's going to be difficult to explain this to the gardener.

d) I wouldn't mind so much but he's got enough pictures of his mother as it is.

e) He says it's because of the antique armoire she's leaning against but we both know it's because of her perfectly waxed floors.

f) It's a strange addition to the country cottage mood board but I'm willing to go with it.

g) He doesn't even realise it's a picture of me.

h) It's disappointing. The *Sunday Times* supplements really aren't what they used to be.

i) Next to the scales. Starting to think my mother was right about him.

j) I really should stop reading *Playboy* to him before we go to bed.

k) Later I find it as his screensaver on his computer. And his phone. And the tablet. Then it's on the fridge and in his calfskin wallet. I find myself cut out of all our wedding photos and replaced by her. By the time I've packed my bags she's all over the entire house. I saw him last week. He was out eating dinner, a cardboard cut-out propped up in the seat opposite him. Everyone was staring.

l) I take down the picture and turn over the tortoise.

ANSWERS
a) Aquarius
b) Aquarius
c) Aquarius
d) Aquarius
e) Replicant
f) Aquarius
g) Aquarius
h) Aquarius
i) Aquarius
j) Aquarius
k) Aquarius
l) Aquarius

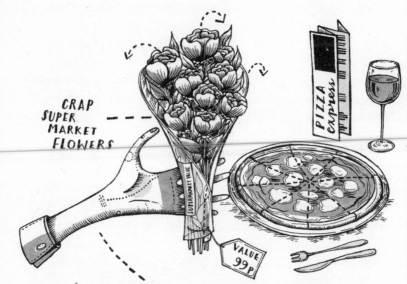

LIBRA BORN 'PEOPLE'

23 SEPTEMBER–23 OCTOBER

Planet: Krypton, originally. Later, Earth. No powers except crushing psychological problems.
Birthstone: Kryptonite. Obviously. As deadly as ever.
Lucky Day: There's got to be one soon, surely?

LIBRA AT A GLANCE

The scales, the only zodiac sign that's neither animal nor man. But that doesn't make Libras any less human. NOTHING could make Libras any less human. The body, yes, but the mind is alien and malleable. Never quite understanding the Earth's potential joys.

An empty husk of a star sign, there is nothing about Libra that is of any interest. Their lives are dull, grey slates on which nothing can be drawn. They offer nothing and take very little. Endless talk of how they put up some shelves at the weekend or telling you about some boring dream that you have to pretend to care about. They are the daytime television of the zodiac. Eamonn Holmes shouting into space about a dog that can do tricks. Philip Schofield introducing this year's winner of *Britain's Got Talent* to a universe of disinterested stars.

Libra's favourite film is *The Shawshank Redemption*. Or *Forrest Gump*. They buy roses for their partner on Valentine's

Day and take them for a candlelit dinner at Pizza Express. They go to the cinema to watch romantic comedies starring Jennifer Aniston. They enjoy doing their ironing at the weekend and consider it a treat to go to Pets at Home. The hardest drug they've ever taken is Calpol and even that was a bit much for them. The most popular name amongst Libras is Colin.

But that's not to say there's no emotion whatsoever. It's ironic that, out of all the signs, Libras are probably the most mentally unbalanced. From their emptiness comes strong and sudden emotional swings. Show a Libra a particularly well-bent paperclip and they'll fall into a joyous rapture usually reserved for when normal people find themselves in bed with someone way above their punching weight. Of course, a well-bent paperclip *is* above a Libra's punching weight.

Libras are the kind of people who let others ahead of them in the queue at McDonald's because of their underlying fear of others. They will not correct shopkeepers when they have been short-changed. Libras are responsible for 90% of albums sold by Coldplay and Mumford & Sons. They will grumble and complain about how their job isn't going anywhere but never make any attempts to get a new one or distinguish themselves from their colleagues in any way.

If you ever want to feel good about yourself (or, more realistically, briefly forget about your life), find a Libra. Show them a bright colour and watch their brow furrow as their brain tries to comprehend something that isn't white, beige or black. Libras are timid, Libras will never get anywhere, Libras are the mopes of the universe.

YOUR YEAR AHEAD

A disconsolate Mars finds a shoulder to cry on in the form of Pluto. They spend more and more time together, their close proximity brings you a good deal of fortune and hope. But, sure enough, Pluto makes a move on Mars and everything gets weird between them. Mars starts to keep its distance from Pluto. The further Mars gets, the worse your life becomes. Pluto's weird and desperate messages on Mars's phone doesn't help matters. Your life is a mess by the end of the year.

January

1–5 You know this is all rubbish, right? I don't mean astrology. I mean life in general.

6–14 There's only so much one person can take. You can't suppress everything. You must release your dark side.

18–20 You are told to watch a hugely popular video today which is apparently 'hilarious'. You don't find it funny.

22–23 They're having an affair, y'know.

24 Your sanity is slowly deteriorating. Each day eats away at you. Each interaction gnawing at what little you have left.

25–30 It's too late. There's nothing you can do.

31 Your enemies don't even have to live well to get their revenge. They just have to live adequately.

Highs: 15–17 You think you see a famous person today but no, it's just someone that looks like them.

Lows: 21 Don't hold back from communicating your feelings. If you can't say it to their face then simply post a bitchy Facebook comment.

February

1 Your mother calls today. No, sorry, just kidding. She still doesn't want anything to do with you.

2–5 It's not paranoia if they're really out to get you! But they're not out to get you. Get over yourself. You're not important.

9–14 You find it quite difficult not to read this as a question?

16–21 The planets have abandoned you. There is no hope.

22 Love finds you today! And proceeds to stamp on your heart.

23 You are fatally wounded today. Hopefully it won't be anything too serious.

24–28 Your boss lectures you on how they always give 100% to everything they do. You quickly sign them up to give blood.

Highs: 6–8 A violent psycho beating your lifeless body is pulled off of you as he screams 'YOU'VE HAD THIS COMING FOR YEARS!' What did you do?

Lows: 15 The mirror, like everyone else, is not your friend today.

March

1–6 You find solace in an obviously ridiculous pseudoscience.

7–13 It's not your wit, confidence and powerful stance that intimidates people, it's the bloodstains . . .

15–18 No, alcohol is not the answer, but it is a pretty good guess.

19–23 After years of self-torture, your paranoia finally pays off. Everyone IS talking about you.

24 You have a brief moment of clarity today and see yourself as you really are. Best to ignore it and forget it ever happened.

27–28 THE COSMIC OWL CONSUMES ALL LIBRAS.

29–30 Men want to be you, women want to be you, dogs want to sniff your bottom. Only the last bit is true.

Highs: 14 It's terminal.

Lows: 31 It isn't clear from the stars if this is about an old PC or a sexual act, but today you must find somewhere to put a 3½ inch floppy.

April

1 You catch someone's eye on the bus today. It's all gooey and disgusting. You should give it back. It sounds like they're in pain.

2–5 Your ticket is called at the Delhi counter of death.

7–10 It's hard to tell your future because the stars keep going out. One by one. Oh, oh God. Run! HIDE!

16–20 Some see your use of foul language as excessive. You see it as necessary.

21–22 Jupiter says you smell and that everybody hates you. Also, Mars called you a 'poo brain'.

23 You slap a stone statue's arse today. You've finally hit rock bottom.

24–26 You're doomed to live a life where your tastes and desires are shaped by the whims of others.

27–30 Who needs nightmares when there's real life?

Highs: 6 Your time at work today makes you die that little bit faster.

Lows: 11–15 You finally get that promotion at work and then realise you're out of your depth. You're soon fired. Know your limits.

May

1–6 You do not pass GO. You definitely don't collect £200.

12–14 Your chances of losing weight are, ironically, slim.

15–19 You are the roadkill on the spiritual highway of life.

20 Your lucky word for today is 'kittens'! Although your unlucky word is 'terrifying wood chipper accident'.

21–23 Your death becomes a day of national celebration in most European countries.

24 This is the first day of the rest of your life. Your miserable, meaningless life.

26–30 You hold your head in your hands hoping for a brief moment of peace from your life. But it's still there for you. Waiting.

31 It's a good job you're not trying to make friends. You're being more hostile than usual.

Highs: 7–11 You're not free. Your mind has been manipulated. Choice is an illusion.

Lows: 25 You meet the love of your life today but you aren't the love of theirs. You never see them again. They forever haunt your memory.

June

1–6 It's out with the old and in with the gnu! New, I meant new. Not suggesting you set up home with a wildebeest.

7 Your Tourette's friend says he'll make you a big fuck off sandwich for lunch today. That's nice.

8 Today, the Goddess of Light appears and informs you that you're mankind's only hope. We don't stand a chance.

9–14 You're so used to it you don't even realise you're constantly crying anymore.

15–20 A giant mutant wasp picks you up and carries you to its underground nest to feed on your guts. Not even your worst day this week.

24–28 Everything happens for a reason. Sometimes, that reason is, you're stupid and make bad choices.

29–30 Venus colludes with Mercury to plan a moment of perfect harmony in all aspects of your life, then forgets to tell anyone.

Highs: 21–22 Your true love in life turns out to be a bag of prawn cocktail crisps.

Lows: 23 You win the Best Fancy Dress Award at the office today – in your usual attire.

July

1–6 Some advice: nothing clears the head like a nice game of Russian Roulette.

7–10 Your volatile nature in social situations is highlighted as a problem. You see it as only a solution.

12–15 You are worthless and everything you try to do will end in failure.

16–20 Your parents finally tell you that they did divorce because of you. It was all your fault after all. The psychiatrist was wrong!

25 You don't intend to come across as cold, dark, sadistic and heartless. But you're happy that you do.

26–30 You're old and getting older. Fat and getting fatter. Sad and getting sadder.

31 You never grew beyond crying when you don't get your own way. It doesn't work on Jupiter.

Highs: 11 You spend today trying to get away with doing as little as possible. A bit like me writing this.

Lows: 21–24 Your taking things way to seriously. I mean, there just grammatical errors.

August

1 You remind me of two of the planets, actually. Saturn Uranus all day, doing nothing exciting.

2–5 You need to become more open to change. Why not become a Leo?

7–10 You are a wandering, lost soul searching for a light to end your dark, lonely misery. It will never come.

11–18 Your internal monologue throws you a curveball by calling you a stain on the freshly laundered shirt of humanity.

20–25 Someone is taking their time over a long term commitment. He'll never marry you. He's already married to Victoria Beckham.

26–31 Some say you drink and swear excessively. You could argue that you don't do it nearly enough.

Highs: 6 The Spanish Inquisition confront you today when you least expect it.

Lows: 19 You lose an argument today as you insist on using logic and common sense. The other person does not.

September

4–8 You try to be sensitive by showing people your true, innermost feelings. This leads to you punching them in the face.

9–14 You're too young to be so angry. But in a world this awful, it's difficult to be anything else.

15 Another day of buying stuff you don't need with money you don't have.

16–20 You don't care about anything. Not one little bit. You can't emphasise how little you care. People just can't comprehend.

25 You see something today. You know where it's been. Yet you still put it in your mouth.

26–29 You fail to avenge your father's death.
30 You will be forgotten long before your death.

Highs: 1–3 Mercury is in retrograde which means it's going in the wrong direction, just like your life.
Lows: 21–24 The little voice in your head is back again. In fact, it's reading this for you. Isn't it?

October
1–4 You are a firework. And everyone else is a lit match. It's inevitable what will happen if they get too close to you.
5 You experience déjà vu today.
14–20 Technology has made it simple for everyone to keep in touch at the click of a button. You use this technology to refuse interaction.
20 Today you treat yourself by pouring a bag of crisps into a bowl before eating them.
21–23 Commence Operation Sudden Death.
24–28 Stop blaming other people. You are the sole cause of all the drama in your life.
29–31 Nice idea. Don't bother.

Highs: 6–14 You may need to do some juggling in your life. You run away to join the circus to escape your miserable existence.
Lows: 5 You experience déjà vu today.

November
1 Today you hulk out and pinch and punch the face of anyone who tells you it's November and that Christmas is next month.
2–5 Doing a good turn, you check for hedgehogs under the bonfire. You trip and fall and get trapped under the wood. Nobody hears your screams.

6–10 Despite the alignment of Venus and Mars, the planet causing your misery is Earth.

11–12 I know it's a big ask, but try not to kill anyone.

18–19 It's the weekend! Or, as you like to call it, lock yourself in your house, close your curtains and binge alone on American TV time!

20–24 You break your leg in a china shop. It gets worse when you're told, thanks to store policy, that you have to buy it.

29–30 It's true that a heart that hurts is a heart that works. But you're dead inside.

Highs: 13–17 When you discover the vowels are up for sale, you don't hesitate. You take two of them without paying and leave an IOU.

Lows: 25–28 Me? I'm fine . . . actually, no, I'm not. You never tell ME what's going to happen in MY life. You're just take, take, take. SELFISH.

December

1 You find a strange and mysterious book in the library called *The Book of Gorax*. It's got strange markings on it. You take it home to study further.

2–7 The illegible writing is somehow becoming clearer. The occasional letter can be read.

8–13 Entire sentences now. They appear to be some form of incantation.

14–20 You can read the entire book easily. You start to hear voices in the night. Noises that wake you up from terrifying dreams.

21–26 An overwhelming urge to say the words is building.

27 Surrounded by candles, you say the words. A sound like the world tearing, cries, moans. Oh, the noise. What have you done?

28–30 There is no escape. Nobody can escape His claws.
31 ALL IS GOOD. ALL IS GORAX.

Highs: Gorax.
Lows: No Gorax.

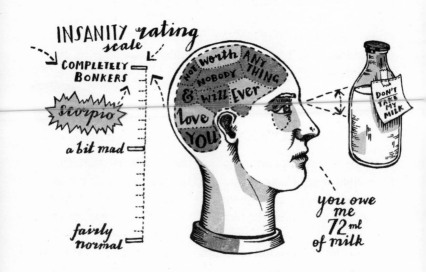

SCORPIO BORN PEOPLE

23 OCTOBER–21 NOVEMBER

Planet: You're lucky to have a home, don't get cocky.
Birthstone: Don't worry, it's just kidney stones. Feel like birthstones though, don't they?
Lucky Day: Nope.

SCORPIO AT A GLANCE

Scorpios are predator arthropods of the Arachnida class. They have eight legs, a pair of strong claws and a segmented tail with a venomous stinger on the end. They range in size from 9 mm to 20 cm. They can be found all over the world in a variety of habitats. Their venom, though dangerous, is rarely fatal. In fact, only about twenty-five of almost 1,750 species are able to mortally injure a human being. Despite this, Scorpios have a reputation as being one of the deadliest of the star signs.

Scorpios, like all the other signs of the zodiac, are not unique. They are not special. They don't have any real marketable skills which they can use to succeed in the world. The best thing that can be said about them is that they're pretty much entirely unnoticeable. As a water sign, Scorpios are overwhelmingly wet. If there's an argument then they will almost certainly back down before it's even properly begun. Scorpios have no backbone.

If a Scorpio listened to their heart they would almost certainly find love but, most of the time, they listen to their head. Specifically the voices that repeat, over and over again, the words 'you're not worth anything and nobody will ever love you'. Scorpios have the highest insanity rate of any sign.

Scorpios like to think they are dynamic, go-getting people but if you ask them to prove it, to actually get up off the settee and do something worthwhile, they won't. They'll just sit there, scratching themselves, pretending to the world that they hate *The Only Way is Essex*. But if you hate it so much, Scorpio, why do you never miss an episode? Why?

They are the pettiest of all the star signs. If you live with a Scorpio and borrow a tiny bit of their milk for your morning cup of tea, expect a passive-aggressive note on the fridge by the time you get home. They will even ensure that they get back the equal amount of milk in the misguided belief they are making some sort of point.

Scorpios are the kind of people who stop in the middle of the street without realising that there are people behind them. They are also likely to get annoyed when said people walk into them. Scorpios are unable to use the really very simple self-serve tills at the supermarket. Scorpios stand on the left-hand side of the escalator. They click their fingers when they want to get the attention of a waiter in a restaurant and never say thank you when a stranger holds open a door for them.

The dream of most Scorpios is to follow in the footsteps of the most famous of all Scorpios. The Scorpio Killer.

YOUR YEAR AHEAD

This year will be one of transition for you as you go from a happy, confident, lucky person into something else entirely.

Let's not go into too much detail as to what that is, we don't want to give away too much, do we? Instead, let's focus on the previous year. One of great stability and happiness filled with love and friendship. It will be these memories that get you through the difficult twelve months ahead.

January

1–4 There's a reason you're having that unavoidable feeling that you're missing out on life.

5–9 You meet a handsome astrologer today and give him your number. Please give him your number. I'm so lonely.

10–13 In the event of an emergency, you won't hesitate to use the nearest person as a human shield.

14–19 You're not, nor will you ever be, anyone's first choice.

21–24 You fake an orgasm in a cafe to see how people react. It's not like the movies. You are barred from the cafe.

25–26 Just when you thought things couldn't get any worse, they do. Much worse.

27 You are a chore to be around.

Highs: 20 People think you've done nothing with your life. You'd prove them wrong if you gave a shit. Or if it wasn't true.
Lows: 28–31 Thanks to your pathologically violent nature, dealing with people kind of sorts itself out.

February

1 The jawbone skitters across the floor. It goes further than you thought it would do.

2–5 THIS IS IT. THIS IS THE END.

6–15 The stars hate you. The planets want you gone. The entire universe will celebrate the day of your demise.

16 A venomous spider laid eggs in your brain last night. I'd advise you to seek medical attention, but it's too late.

17–24 Single? Remember, you're single by choice. It's just not your choice.

26 So many challenges to face today, take them one at a time. Right shoe goes on *right* foot.

27 You get drunk tonight and text your exes. But they're dead. All of them dead.

Highs: 25 Today is the pinnacle of your life. Which just confirms how pathetic your life has been, and inevitability, will be.

Lows: 28 Today is brought to you by the words 'Oh God', 'no' and 'please, don't'.

March

1–9 The fast-paced lifestyle isn't for you. You would have liked to be born 200 years ago. Mainly because you'd be dead by now.

10–11 You can't change the past. But if you get drunk enough, you won't remember the past. So, it never actually happened.

12–16 If you did have a gun in your pocket, you would be happy to see some people.

17–18 Hell is other people. And the other people are in your mind. Telling you to do things.

20 You find yourself doing that funny run as you cross the road today. It doesn't help you avoid the oncoming traffic.

21–26 Everything dies. Why should your dreams be any different?

28–31 You travel back in time only to discover you have nothing to teach the people in the past.

Highs: 19 Some work colleagues treat you like family. They only talk to you when they want something and you try to avoid them at costs.

Lows: 27 Someone on the bus today loudly plays that song you love. No, just kidding, that's NEVER going to happen.

April

1 Your future today isn't worth telling.

2–8 Your use of technology is lessening your humanity. But at least you don't have to talk to people as much.

9–13 To solve hostility, you need to be the bigger person and bury the hatchet right in their face.

14 You go for a meal tonight with someone from the stock exchange and play FTSE under the table.

16 Jupiter pops round for tea later but you serve own brand biscuits. Expect heavy retribution.

17–20 He isn't coming back, Scorpio. He isn't coming back.

21–29 You only exist in the subliminal dimensions of time.

Highs: 15 You find love in an unexpected place today and you just know the doctors won't believe the story of how it got up there.

Lows: 30 Today is one of those days where you'll be lucky not to appear on the news. On a national scale.

May

1–8 Your mother is so fat. That's it.

9 You meet someone who actually believes in horoscopes today. They say things like 'typical Leo' and mean it. It's confusing.

17 Make the most of today, it could be your last. It won't be. Probably.

18–20 You enjoy witnessing a person taking a selfie. It's nice to be reminded that others are lonely too.

21 You dance like no one is watching. Because no one ever watches you. Ever. Regardless of what you're doing.

23 You sepnd all day spttoing spelilng miastkes erveywehre. It's all in yuor haed.

24–31 Single? I suggest you dramatically lower your standards. Lower. And lower. And again. Keep going.

Highs: 10–16 You subconsciously sabotage any chance of happiness you may have because you love moaning and complaining so much.

Lows: 22 Nothing for you today.

June

1 You accomplish nothing today. You don't learn anything, you don't meet anybody new. Nothing. A complete waste of time.

2–8 Stop that. It's disgusting.

10–16 That shadow in your room is getting bigger and darker and starting to look hungry. It's waiting at the foot of the bed.

17–19 Euuuurrrggghhhhaaaarrrggghhhhh.

20 A gnawing, intense desperation reduces you to reading your horoscope for some sort of vague and meaningless answer.

22–26 Today your relationship ensures your awful day doesn't have to end at work.

27–30 A good fart will give you all the space you need.

Highs: 9 There's only one thing that annoys you today. Sadly that one thing is everything.

Lows: 21 The growth on your back you've been ignoring begins to talk today. It tells you to do things. Bad things. Things with fire.

July

1–9 FLIES. MILLIONS AND MILLIONS OF FLIES.

11 The doctor has bad news for you today. They've been sleeping with your partner. And you have cancer.

12–19 Looking back, historians will see your actions as mankind's lowest point.

20 This is probably the most you've ever cried in one day, right?

22–26 If you're happy and you know it and you really want to show it, if you're happy and you know it keep it to yourself.

27–31 You'll need a sharp knife, lipstick, the top hat from a Monopoly set and a REALLY good alibi.

Highs: 10 Your future seems fine until about 3 p.m. Then there's a bright flash, then nothing . . .

Lows: 21 You sign an Internet petition today. Good one, bet you feel pretty good about yourself. Making all the changes.

August

2–9 Every day is a gift. Although in your case it's the gift you quietly exchange for vouchers.

10 'It could've been worse' isn't the greatest defence but, after your actions this morning, it's the best one you've got.

12 Today doesn't kill you. And it also doesn't make you stronger. If anything, it weakens you.

13 Imagine going to the Love Shack, but realising you've left your jukebox money at home. Today will be a bigger disappointment.

14–21 You accidentally talk about Fight Club.

22–26 You're late for work because deep down you don't respect your job or anyone you work with.

27–31 Quick! Look! Oh, you missed it. Now! It's back! Nope, missed it again.

Highs: 1 The moon is in your Second House today. (Two houses? One of them big enough to hold the moon? Show-off).

Lows: 11 You're not sure whether that smell on the bus today is coming from you or somebody else.

September

1–6 Mars is in retrograde and Mercury is eclipsed by Venus. Well, not really. But it's not like you were going to check.

7 Today you replace the can of air freshener in the workplace lavatory with an air horn. So now it's just a waiting game.

9–12 You don't agree with putting your hands up in the air like you just don't care. Because you never care. Your arms would be very tired.

13–19 Look at it this way. Now this way. And, finally, how is it this way? It's not right, is it? Seek medical advice.

21–26 You will never have enough money and freedom to do what you really want with your life.

27 You chop vegetables with the Grim Reaper today. You're dicing with Death.

28–30 Smell the morning air. Take a deep breath. Inhale the spores, let them dig in. Deeper.

Highs: 8 Your dog loses its nose today and the wound gets infected. How does it smell? Like an infected dog's nose. Awful.

Lows: 20 You find yourself a shoulder to cry on when you break down on the motorway and weep for hours beside your vehicle.

October

1 You see a ninja today who isn't very good at his job.

2 Venus makes your life a misery today. Serena isn't too kind to you either. Tennis has changed those two.

3–9 It becomes evident early on that you don't have the time or patience to suffer the business of others.

11–15 They're talking about promotions at work and your name is mentioned followed by hysterical, frantic laughter.

16 The conjunction of Venus and Pluto today makes you late for work. But try explaining that to your boss.

17–24 Do you ever feel like you don't belong and have no purpose? Well you're right.

26–31 One day you'll have children and all you'll have to pass on to them is the bitterness and regret over your own life choices.

Highs: 10 You're feeling lonely and vulnerable but soon a friend will be round. Though I don't know how them being a circle will help.

Lows: 25 The memories of today are already starting to fade. What a waste of your time.

November

1–7 ERROR 40404. Astral plane not found. If you think this astral plane should be here, please contact your universe provider.

8 Today the 'L' in your luck has been replaced with an 'F'.

10 HORSES DESCEND ON YOU TODAY.

11–16 Billions of locusts gather to form a giant hand. It points at you. You are singled out and devoured.

17–21 Don't worry, death is only the beginning. Of a never-ending pain.

23–30 Mars rising means you have no chance of chatting up the beautiful stranger on the train. Yeah, keep blaming Mars.

Highs: 9 The greatest torture you can receive is being left to live your life uninterrupted.

Lows: 22 There was a knife-wielding psychotic maniac standing over your sleeping body. He'll be back.

December

1 At lunchtime, you overhear a strange conversation between two short, hairy men. 'He is coming,' they say. 'Gather everyone you can, we return to the ground.' You don't think much of it at the time.

2–8 You see the two men again and, out of curiosity, spend a few days following them. They are stocking up on tinned food and other supplies. You hear the word 'Gorax' but you have no idea what it means.

9–14 You decide to talk to them. They are Mole People. They tell you of the coming of the Destroyer and, taking pity on you, invite you to join them. You laugh it off and carry on at work. Christmas is coming, after all.

15–18 A nagging feeling in the back of your head. There's a strange and worrying atmosphere everywhere you go.

19–20 You see them again and ask if it isn't too late to join them. They say no, so you tell a very small number of friends and gather your supplies.

21–28 There are hundreds of you hiding in a huge cave network deep underground. Defences are built, food is rationed. Children, not knowing the extent of the danger, play and laugh. Their sounds empty and hollow.

29 From the surface high above you hear a terrifying noise like an air raid siren slowed down and amplified. The ground shakes occasionally but the caves hold.

30 Distant screams. The noises sound like they're getting closer somehow. But they couldn't, surely? Not this far under the Earth?

31 The last thing you see is a huge claw ripping open the ceiling. It's . . . it's awful.

Highs: Becoming one with Gorax.
Lows: Not realising you're being digested.

CELEBRITY READING: JEREMY CLARKSON

Jeremy Clarkson, born on 11 April 1960, is an Aries who has the moon and the other, secret moon (due to reveal itself in July) as his two rulers. Aries is a traditionally loud-mouthed sign and Jeremy is no different. His love of cars is caused by the sun's ascendancy in the eighteenth cycle of Capricorn and Scorpio mixed together in a cosmic blender (£18, see catalogue). Saturn descending into the seventh adjacency conjoined with Venus discovering its inner beauty will have no effect on Jeremy whatsoever.

In May, Jeremy will make some rather choice remarks about one of the planets in his newspaper column. 'Wind farms,' writes Jeremy, 'Are about as useful as Jupiter on a snooker table.' It isn't the greatest turn of speech but, then again, Aries have never been known for their skills with words. Does he mean that the planet is too big to use a snooker ball? That the weight of the gas giant will crush the table and everyone currently playing? Nobody knows. Anyway.

Jupiter doesn't take kindly to the words and teams up with Mars and Pluto to slowly influence Jeremy's life into less than positive directions. By June, Jeremy can be seen walking around the streets of Hampstead holding two pieces of cardboard crudely cut out in the shape of a car. In August, he will be videoed riding a paper horse, wearing a tin pot as a helmet and charging, again and again, the wind farms of Cornwall.

The stars seem to be reporting that Richard Hammond will be nearby, riding a donkey and dreaming of a governorship. The planets, taking pity on Jeremy, will cease their meddling and after two months of privacy, he will be free to continue his life.

Interestingly, with the planets leaving Jeremy alone, he discovers that he is the only truly free man in the world. Perhaps even the only free man to have ever lived. Thinking for himself for the first time, he renounces fast cars and controversial opinions and dedicates his life to building yurts in trendy suburbs of north London. The planet Mars, a big fan of *Top Gear*, decides to interfere in order to get Jeremy back on the air. However, Mercury, which cannot stand the programme, tries to counter the movements of Mars in order to keep Clarkson in one of his many yurts. The planets' efforts have disastrous effects and instances of severe flooding increase throughout the last quarter of the year.

A number of environmental groups realise what is going on and are faced with a dilemma. Do they help their enemy Jeremy Clarkson back on the air or do they allow tens of thousands of lives to be ruined by severe flooding caused by the movements of the fighting planets? What do they do? Tune in next year to find out!

Right, so listen up, it's come to my attention through the psychic waves of the universe that someone, some woman I used to date, is going to put some adverts in here that say I'm not the real deal.

Well, if I was making this up how would I know what she's going to do?

Don't answer, I already know what you're going to say, I'm a psychic. I don't use those cheap tricks that the other 'psychics' have. I don't have stooges, I don't have secret questionnaires, I don't have a brother that works in the place they print this thing who feeds me information before they go to press.

So, this woman, Katharine. Yeah, her and I dated for a bit but did I propose to her?

Just good old-fashioned, honest-to-goodness psychic abilities.

Did I really lead her down the marriage route?

She's **crazy**. Of course she's crazy. She was obsessed with me, never left me alone. Always calling late at night when I wasn't at her flat like I said I would be. We weren't exclusive, it's not my fault if she thought we were. She wanted kids or something, I don't know. She went all jealous if I looked at the text I got from a woman I'd met in a bar the previous night. It was all too intense. You know how it is guys.

Here's a reading for you. **Beware** the woman who seems really cool at first but stops putting out after a few weeks because 'you've had too much to drink'. **Beware** the woman who calls your ex-girlfriend and shouts down the phone just because she found out you'd been calling her most nights that week. **Beware** the woman who gets angry when she finds the hidden folder on your computer full of pictures of her friends which you saved from Facebook.

For all other queries, don't hesitate to contact me,

Edward Treason

at the usual address.
I can help you turn your life around.

As long as you're not called Katharine.

Personal readings from Horrorscopes !
Don't call us! We'll call you!
Or even come round to your house!
WE KNOW WHERE YOU LIVE.

Your own personal astrological reading!

Here at Horrorscopes we've learnt how to condense thousands of years of wisdom, learning and expertise into one easy to charge for automated telephone service. Simply dial the usual number for access to the pre-recorded secrets of your future!

Our unique system devised over literally six weeks of study breaks up every possible future and narrows them down to just **twelve potential outcomes.** Every single Libra in the entire world, approximately 600,000,000 of them, will all receive the same reading because all of their futures have been ordained by the same set of stars! It sounds impossible to believe, doesn't it?

BUT IT'S TRUE!

And for only £30 you can get a unique Horrorscopes book that's personal only to you and the millions of other people who share your sign!

● Readings that go into excruciating amounts of detail about which moon you were born under on the seventh day of the fourth house of Aquarius and what this means for your future (hint: it means EVERYTHING)!

● In-depth profiles which explain the true nature of both yourself, how you connect in a deeper sense to the planet and the theme tune to that television programme you loved as a kid that you've never been able to remember!

● A personal forecast! All the same as the above but worded slightly differently and with a further emphasis on how the sun, rotating in a quarterly direction at the time of your birth, can possibly, or possibly not, help you to a better tomorrow!

SAGITTARIUS BORN PEOPLE

22 NOVEMBER–21 DECEMBER

Planet: Logic says yes, science says NO.
Birthstone: Gritting salt.
Lucky Day: Any day you actually wake up sober before
    2 p.m.

SAGITTARIUS AT A GLANCE

Due to the height of Mercury's sun in the twenty-first quadrant
of the gamma universe, Sagittarians are passionate, exciting
and full of life. They have a good sense of humour and a
natural connection to the Earth. They are the most spiritual of
all the signs and also gullible enough to believe all of the
above because it says something nice about them.

They are the sign that's likely to consider themselves
creative despite the fact that all their ideas come from half-
remembered adverts or the plots of books they've read about
on Wikipedia. In fact, almost all of their knowledge comes
from Wikipedia. On surface level, a Sagittarian will appear to
be well informed on a huge range of topics but, if you press
them, you'll find nothing of any depth.

Sagittarians, when you meet them in the pub and give them
your number, will lead you on and let you think you have a
chance before stomping on your heart. They don't understand

what it's like. Why didn't she give me a chance? Why? Is one date too much to ask? One date to prove that it could've worked out?

The main aspect of Sagittarians is their luck. They often walk into jobs they don't necessarily deserve purely because they went to school with somebody who works there. They always get the last potato of a Sunday roast or the final ticket to that concert you wanted to go to. However, the worst thing about them is that Sagittarians are so damn nice. Despite everything, all the reasons why they should be too annoying to even consider, you can't help but like them.

Don't get too confident though, Sagittarius. This is ultimately one of the worst personality types in amongst the entire zodiac. Your sheer jamminess has led to a drop in standards that can never be reversed. Previously, people in your position would have got there by skill and hard work. Nowadays, with your connections getting you everywhere, mediocrity has taken over. Your overall lack of anything approaching expertise means your work is bland and uninspired. You are the problem, Sagittarius. You.

If Sagittarians aren't stopped then it will soon be too late. We must all rise against them, to see through their money-soaked charisma and reclaim the world they have taken over. But we won't. Unable to put aside our petty differences, Sagittarius will continue its takeover. We are doomed to a life of white electronic devices, flat-pack furniture and fifteen types of beige paint on our walls.

YOUR YEAR AHEAD

Last year you were constantly dealing with the unexpected and you dealt with it well. Sadly, this year you've simply run out of energy. It's one problem after another, Sagittarius, and you're just not mentally strong enough to deal with it anymore. A slight change in your bill payments? Tears. A couple of new, slightly more difficult tasks at work? Screaming and shouting. Falling behind on your rent or mortgage? Complete breakdown. On the bright side, you have done well to get this far in life, it's just a pity you won't be going much further.

January

1 You order a Domino's pizza today and subsequently break a tooth on double-six.

2–7 Release the hounds.

8–12 The sports team/man/woman you support/vaguely follow/despise wins/doesn't win today/soon/at some point.

14 You think you fancy an electrician today but there's just no spark between you.

15–18 Your doctor informs you that you have a tragic case of progressive Mick Hucknalling of the face.

19 Today, you cut off your nose to spite your face. And as an excuse to feel something. Anything.

20–24 Your luck's about to change! It's going to get even worse.

Highs: 13 You make friends with someone beautiful today. But just friends. Again.

Lows: 25–31 You are way past your 'best before' date.

February

1 An age-old argument will be resolved today when you get to shake hands with the Queen.

2 You triumph with an impossible, yet epic throw of rubbish into a distant bin. The highlight of your day. Nobody sees it.

8 Pluto is doing a double cosmic twinkle and doors will open for you today. (No, they're NOT automatic doors; that's PlutoPower™).

9–15 The minute you walked in the joint, I could see you would be barred from the carvery . . .

16 You are in conflict with another sign today. The sign is, well, all of them. Including your own. Everyone is intolerable.

17–24 Your imaginary friend finds someone new to hang out with.

Highs: 3–7 You can't fathom how to measure the depth of water.

Lows: 25–28 You discover that your pet goldfish, Steve, is your only friend in the world. Steve hates you. Steve spreads rumours about you.

March

1 A&E first thing today, then Argos for a new hoover.

2–8 Stop that. I can see you.

9–13 You bake a cake for your Nan's 100th birthday. It poisons her. What's wrong with you?

14 You spend four and a half hours at work Googling tips on how to be more productive.

19 Today you invest everything in a company that manufactures inflatable skulls, only for it to blow up in your face.

20–26 Lorem ipsum dolor sit amet, consectetur adipiscing elit. Vestibulum a nunc sapien. Quisque posuere iaculis aliquet.

Highs: 15–18 You end years of speculation by finally admitting it was you who let the dogs out.

Lows: 27–31 Tattoo regret.

April

1 You get the feeling you're being patronised today. But try not to worry your pretty little head about it.

2–9 It'll happen before you hear it. And then black, eternal nothingness.

10 The last thing you expected today was to go out for dinner with a supermodel. You were right not to expect it. You eat alone again.

11–14 With your quick temper, people won't like you when you're angry. Or in any other circumstances.

15 You're late for work today. Although, in your case, 'work' means 'the afternoon repeats of *Diagnosis Murder*'.

16–19 You focus on an old relationship when you drunkenly message your ex on Facebook and ask if they still love you.

20 Today you will get home and take the dog out. One shot, back of the head.

Highs: 21 Your experiment with LSD has no negative effects on you today. But you do end up owing money to a mermaid on a unicorn.

Lows: 22–30 You're off work! Being made redundant will have that effect . . .

May

1 You get bitten by a radioactive human today. You don't get any superpowers but you do get a slow and painful death.

2 You will self-destruct in five seconds.

13 You draw a lot of money at the bank today, but they won't accept it.

14–21 Everything has changed. Black is white. White is black. This may have a negative impact on your life.

22–30 You update a favourite phone app and it no longer works. Though this is less of prediction and more of a certainty.

Highs: 3–12 You've spent so long watching football that the commentators' clichés are taking over your life. Anyway, go out there and give it 110%.

Lows: 31 A colleague's professional life improves drastically today when you're fired for gross misconduct.

June

1 Well well well, it's someone's lucky day! Not yours, obviously. Yours was last month. You slept through it.

2–7 If you want to live, don't look behind you. Don't. Just walk away.

8 Trouble today, as the Democratic Republic of Congo declares war on you.

16 Trying to be cool, you write 'Fo' Pa' in your dad's Father's Day card. I think that's a mistake.

23 Today you make first contact with an alien life form and, well, you've never been good at first impressions, have you?

24–30 FIRE AND DEATH. And cupcakes! But, more importantly, CUPCAKES!

Highs: 9–15 Cupid draws back his bow, and lets his arrow go, straight to your lover's heart. You're charged with being an accessory to murder.

Lows: 17–22 You're disappointed that your partner doesn't comment on your new haircut. But you're more disappointed that they left you years ago.

July

1–6 Your marriage is loveless and imaginary.

7 Finally! Someone sends you a message on OKCupid! But, no, they don't meet your unrealistically high standards.

8–14 You avoid smoking to decrease the chance that cancer will kill you. Unfortunately, today a giant crab kills you.

15–18 A close advisor finds something more important than you to worr . . . oh, hey, a squirrel!

19 You get more than you bargained for today when you bargain for something and get more then you anticipated.

20–24 If you're happy and you know it, I'd be very surprised.

Highs: 22 You try to impress mates by putting a lime in a coconut. No coconut, so you use a cup. No mates either. Alone, you put a lime in a cup.
Lows: 25–31 They've found you. Run. Run now.

August

1–4 You regret putting up 'Wanted: Dead or Alive' posters for your lost dog.

5 HUNDREDS OF BIRDS SWARM, THEY CARRY US ALL AWAY TO OUR DOOM. TO BIRD CITY, THEY SQUAWK. TO BIRD CITY.

6 Today isn't the greatest. But at least you have your health. The slowest form of death.

8–12 You're approached by a photographer who says you would be perfect for his latest project. He's looking for 'before' pictures.

13 You receive a phone call from your partner but don't finish the conversation as you're breaking up. Good phone signal though.

14–23 You've only just realised you're naked.

Highs: 7 A productive day – after weeks of trying you finally find the end of the sellotape.
Lows: 24–31 You are found wanting.

September

1–7 They say that truth is stranger than fiction. That's not true in your case. A book about your life would be very dull.

8 You wake up crying, you will go to bed crying.

9 A spelling error on an application form makes your life awkward today as a lardy boy from Thailand arrives at your door.

10–15 You would never stand by and watch whilst anyone goes through difficulties. Unless it's funny, of course – in which case film it.

16 Having warmed them up for a few days, you turn the dial on your weather machine to 'BOIL THE OCEANS'.

18 You get up, go to work, come home, TV, sleep, go to work. £25k in student fees . . .

Highs: 17 An embarrassing moment when you get caught in your flies today. I don't know what's worse, the pain or the disgusted looks from the other fishermen.
Lows: 19–30 You open up to a complete stranger. Or 'indecent exposure', as the police call it.

October

1–8 You see a dog licking its genitals. You wonder if you could do that. But its owner won't let you near.

9–15 You become emotional arguing over the most efficient way to rip up pieces of paper. It will end in tears.

17–20 You experience an all-consuming feeling of existential dread. Fortunately you find a spare toilet roll next to the cistern.

21 Today you're trampled to death by an elephant. Yeah, it's a little unusual but don't blame me, it's the moon and the planets and that.

23–31 So much could happen to you. I was studying the stars last night. There's loads of them. They could mean anything.

Highs: 16 Your phone nearly runs out of battery but you get to a charger in time and it's fine. Still. Bit tense for a moment there.

Lows: 22 You get stressed today when trying to figure out what 'desserts' says backwards.

November

1–8 You become hugely famous by breaking the record for the largest intake of helium. Try to keep your feet on the ground.

9–14 You realise that not everybody sees 'dad' as a mythical creature that'll come home one day.

15 On the 479th consecutive day of wearing them, for some reason your 'lucky pants' fail you yet again.

16–17 It takes much careful deliberation before you decide whether to say your piece. I wouldn't bother – nobody is interested.

18 Today you become the first person ever truly abandoned by God.

20 You think about MySpace for the first time in ages today. Still don't log on though.

Highs: 19 It takes you two attempts before you manage to plug in a USB device correctly.

Lows: 21–30 You lose your job at the jelly factory after throwing a wobbler at your boss.

December

1 A strange package arrives for you at work. It is marked simply 'Sagittarius'. Inside it is the address of an old abandoned warehouse just outside of town and a note saying '6 p.m. tomorrow'.

2 There are hundreds of people at the warehouse all standing around and waiting to find out what's going on. Eventually, a man stands up at the side of the room, his voice echoes throughout the building. 'Sagittarians!' he shouts. 'The end is coming and only we can stop it.' He tells of the end days, how he's brought you all there to train for the fight against something called 'Gorax'. Half the people leave but you stay, there's something about him you believe. You decide to join him.

3–27 Training. Agility, balance, speed, weapons, everything. After just over three weeks the man calls you all together. 'Tomorrow, he arrives,' he says. 'Together, we can defeat him.' Everybody cheers.

28 A noise wakes you all up the next morning. It is hellish, like a thousand crying babies. You all pick up your weapons and leave the warehouse.

29 It's huge. You fight, many of you fall but you survive the day. It walks, oh God it walks, but you are certain that the fight can be won.

30 Something's different. Yesterday your attacks worked, some of you got through, but now it's as if the creature knows of your moves before you do them. Hundreds, thousands of Sagittarians lie dead. You barely escape back to the base before trying again tomorrow.

31 The roof of the warehouse is torn open and Gorax pours fire into your rooms. How did it know? It is too late to find out.

Highs: Meeting your fellow man, working together for a shared goal. A real sense of community.
Lows: Seeing that community torn apart by Gorax.

CAPRICORN BORN PEOPLE

22 DECEMBER–19 JANUARY

Planet: Mercury, until March when you, like, totally hear that it kissed Brad at the party and you're, like, 'Oh my God Mercury knew I was into Brad I can't believe it did this to me that planet is dead to me'.

Birthstone: The cold, cold stone you call your heart.

Lucky Day: 29 February.

CAPRICORN AT A GLANCE

Your most noticeable qualities, Capricorn, are elements of negativity, pessimism, cynicism and self-loathing. You are not a fun person to be around. Nevertheless, it says on my chart that Capricorns are the sexiest of all of the zodiac signs but, going by the others, that's not saying much.

Anger isn't necessarily a bad trait to have. It has been used as a great motivator for good and necessary causes. When directed properly, it can be a fine and noble part of somebody's personality. However, and I think you knew this was coming, you often direct your anger at the smallest things. For example, in June this year, when you find the toilet roll hung incorrectly, that's hardly a cause for the £500 worth of damage that follows.

You're a difficult sign to get to know or, at least, that's what you tell yourself. Keep on believing that the effect of Mars in your solar orbit means it takes a while before you're comfortable with people. That's why nobody comes round to your place. It's either that or face up to the fact that nobody really wants to get to know you.

Capricorns were the most ambitious sign until they discovered the allure of television box sets. Their once great promise is now reduced to twelve-hour marathon sessions of *Breaking Bad*, *The Wire* or any of the other long-running television dramas. They convince themselves that they'll only watch a few episodes before getting down to something worthwhile but the next thing they know it's five in the morning and they have to get up for work in two hours. The closest thing to introspection that a Capricorn gets is when they finish a series and come face to face with their lives for an hour or two. Then they start watching *The Sopranos* for a sixth time.

Punctuality would usually be a positive trait but not for Capricorn. These are people who are always on time. If a non-Capricorn is running late to meet a Capricorn, they know the latter will already be waiting for them. It's annoying, Capricorn. Especially the way you say it's all right when we both know it isn't. I mean, come on. It wouldn't be so bad if you got openly annoyed but the way you smile and pretend everything's okay? Ugh. Stop it.

Capricorns are frightened of very little except love, kindness and compassion. When faced with such positive mindsets, you immediately shut down emotionally and pretend that they aren't happening. You rarely seek help despite the fact that you so obviously need it. You're a constant mess, Capricorn. You're a state. Sort yourself out.

YOUR YEAR AHEAD

This is a year of transition for you. Last year was great; it felt like you had it all. A loving partner, an amazing job and plenty of friends who would have done anything for you. And then you got drunk, didn't you? Really, *really* drunk. You can't even remember what you said but it must've been something spectacularly awful. You woke up on New Year's Day outside your home, no idea how you got there and nothing but your pyjamas and a Roxy Music LP for company. This year, you and the LP will form a crime-fighting duo (Pyjamas For Your Pleasure!) solving the problems of the homeless but it's going to be a long year until you reach that level of success.

January

1–6 Snakes. SNAKES. Oh my God, the snakes.

7–10 The bodies are found.

11 Today [raise hope] [planet] [insult disguised as compliment] [crush all dreams into a bottomless pit of eternal dark reality].

15–19 Not even God could help. And there is no God. Only chaos. Good luck!

20–24 A perfect opportunity arises to catch up with neighbours. You've got a month's worth to watch on your Sky+.

26 You get drunk and text your exes. But they're dead. All of them dead.

27 Today you select the wrong eyebrow hair to pluck and your face collapses like a game of Kerplunk.

28–31 Good news! There's no bad news. Bad news. Nothing ever happens to you.

Highs: 12–14 If you're not going to make any efforts to improve your life, I'm not going to bother reading your future.
Lows: 25 You decide to go camping after hearing someone say that passion is an intense emotion.

February

1–4 Whatever it is, get over it. Nobody cares about your problems.

5–10 Everybody hates you.

11–13 You don't want emotions. The only ones you feel hurt you. But they're the only ones you deserve.

15 Typical. You've never ever been run over by a bus before and then today three run you over at once.

16–21 You need a better pick-up method than those elaborate diagrams showing the difference between the Picard and Ryker manoeuvres.

22–26 You meet someone who'll become a vital part of your life. He'll become your lawyer.

28 You fall in love four times on the way to work this morning. None of them are even remotely aware of you.

Highs: 27 The universe has better things to do than control the minutiae of your life.

Lows: 14 Concerned by the rain, you build an ark. You take two of every animal. The ark collapses under the weight, and everyone drowns.

March

1–9 Life is just easier when you're drunk.

10–13 Getting the same morning bus as them for three years without saying anything doesn't count as a long-term relationship.

14–16 You invent a cure for death, but are tragically killed before you have a chance to tell anyone about it.

17 At first today feels just like any other day, and then it is, and then you go to bed.

19 You'll have some much needed time to yourself tonight as your friends fail to invite you on their annual holiday to Ibiza.

20–25 Judging by your Tesco 'Bag For Life', you've got about a week left.

26–31 Your high opinion of yourself is based entirely in fantasy.

Highs: 18 You realise you've exhausted OKCupid, *Guardian* Soulmates and Tinder. Now it's just a choice between the real world or lifelong loneliness.

Lows: 22 You're looking good. No, seriously. Well, quite good. From a distance. If you squint.

April

1–7 Someone ruins the ending HE WAS DEAD ALL ALONG of *The Sixth Sense* for you.

8 BRING OUT THE GIMP!

15–18 You decide to treat yourself which, as you're a brain surgeon, is an incredibly bad idea.

19–22 Life is a case of mind over matter. I don't mind, and you don't matter.

23–24 Make an effort to get to know a newcomer to your area. They're both rich and elderly.

25 You wake up this morning to find yourself transformed into a gigantic insect. Nobody notices.

26–30 Your body is crumbling as your heart turns to dust. Every day is another loveless day towards death.

Highs: 9–11 Your constant negativity makes you a chore to be around.

Lows: 12–14 It's nice that you finally have a friendly office nickname but it's a pity it's 'the creepy one who I think is going to ask me out'.

May

1–4 DEATH.

5–9 Today, you find yourself touched for the very first time in a place you didn't even know existed.

10–15 You realise today that you take most of your life advice from the lady on your SatNav.

16–17 Jupiter helps you get closer to where you want to be as the new secretary at work actually believes in this astrology nonsense.

18–20 You turn someone's frown upside-down today and are promptly arrested for mutilating their face.

21 You're not sure about the new 'Blood Sacrifice Thursday' idea at work today.

22–28 Waiting, the sort of fear you haven't felt since you were five. Old and dead memories surface like bloated bodies.

Highs: 29–30 You don't think it would be fair to single out anyone. So you just agree to hating everyone equally.

Lows: 31 You are finally found out today as the chancer you've always been.

June

1 You go through today with a constant feeling of inner emptiness.

6–10 Your own poor decisions have more of an effect on your life than the planets ever will.

16 Jupiter's orbit around the sun causes you to keep on hitting yourself. 'Why are you hitting yourself?' booms the planet.

17–20 You meet someone today and instantly realise how you wish to spend the rest of your life. Without them in it.

21–25 Well, this is it. Death. I'd say you had a good innings but I can't bring myself to lie to the dying.

26 Your addiction to drama will destroy every positive relationship you've ever had.

27–28 Each year the average human will be swallowed in their sleep by eight separate spiders.

29–30 They'll be here soon.

Highs: 2–5 Your world SEND US MONEY is filled DESTROY PIERS MORGAN with subliminal messages today.

Lows: 11–15 Your uncle kills your father with a herd of bison . . . no, wait, that's *The Lion King* again.

July

1–9 Not even the mighty power of the planets can prevent the stray bullet from piercing your heart.

10–13 The butterfly effect is demonstrated when the COSMIC BUTTERFLY flaps its wings and a tidal wave crushes your home.

15–17 You are all alone.

18–20 Good news! The position of Pluto means you get that promotion! Bad news. Astrology is meaningless.

22–26 The collision of Mars and Earth has a negative impact on your life.

27–30 It's not worth the jail time. It's not worth the jail time. It's not worth the jail time. It's not worth the jail time.

31 Oh God, so much blood . . .

Highs: 21 You're arrested for a crime you didn't commit but, to be fair, you have got away with loads of illegal stuff that you did do.

Lows: 14 You spend far too much time today considering why a dog looks naked without its collar.

August

1–4 You receive a boost when someone gives you a Cadbury Boost.

5–8 You manage to complete your usual tasks at work in half the normal time. Probably because you do them very badly.

11–18 You feel like an idiot today when you have to make a 180-degree turn while walking in public.

19–24 Don't let anyone talk you out of doing what you want. If you want to play cribbage with that gibbon again, just do it.

25–28 You find love! No, hang on, that's not love. It's half an apple. Still, for you, that's not bad.

29 And once you've pulled them all out today, your teeth can be used for ineffective magic rituals.

30 If you work hard enough today, your dreams can come true. Not the nice dreams. The dark and formless ones. Just imagine their screams.

Highs: 9–10 You are nothing. NOTHING.
Lows: 31 You accidentally insult Noel Fielding and he attacks you with a ghost made of awful and pointless non-sequiturs.

September

1–3 Your tests come back positive. I'm so sorry.

4–10 The longer the day goes on, the more violence becomes the only reasonable and logical outcome.

11–15 As one door closes, another one opens. Lovely proverb, it's just a shame you're in a room with only one door.

17–20 Now's the moment for you need to deal with your low self-esteem issues, you drippy, pathetic loser.

21–26 Don't let your shyness put you off telling someone how much you like them. Why not text them? Once every ten minutes.

27 Not good enough.

28–30 There is no light strong enough to pierce the darkness of your life.

Highs: 16 You murder David Essex in a lift . . . sorry, my chart's upside down. You get a lift to Essex with a murderer called David.

Lows: 22–27 You're wasting the little time you have left.

October

4 You fall in love with a stranger on the train today. They would've said yes if you asked them out. Coward. No happiness for you.

5–10 You get ill after eating German food. Your doctor says he fears the wurst.

16–20 Nobody notices when your body goes missing.

21–22 You think you feel your phone vibrate in your pocket but no, nobody's made an effort to talk to you.

23–25 I'd say it's a shame that your partner's left you but it's for the best. For them, that is. They achieve loads without you.

26–30 I know everyone is supposed to be beautiful in some form. But no. Not you.

31 Somebody disagrees with you today so you spend all day moaning to other people about it when they're not around.

Highs: 1–3 A wondering zebra never blinks, even during a storm. Think about that, think hard.

Lows: 11–15 It's no surprise that you hate your life.

November

1–6 Like a game of Tetris, all the pieces of your life are falling into pla . . . OH GOD, I can't believe you put that block there. You're ruined.

8–10 The rope holds.

11–13 You flick a coin into a wishing well today and it instantly reimburses you. It doesn't want to give you false hope.

14–17 If you love the stars so much why don't you just marry them?

18–20 You see a beautiful person and your heart skips a beat. Then it goes into full cardiac arrest. Not your best pick-up move.

21 Today could see you bag that dream job. Could, but won't.

25–30 Stop crying, pull yourself together. You're a mess.

Highs: 7 Jupiter rises in your house. With your mum.
Lows: 22–24 A brief moment of self-awareness reveals what a disappointment you are to your family.

December

1 You get the last parking space in the lot. Amazing. Good work.

2–9 Things are looking up! Your boss calls you in and tells you you're going to be promoted in January!

10–14 It gets better! A beautiful, *beautiful* person asks you out on your way to work, you go on a first date and everything goes perfectly. You sly old dog, you.

15–24 Oh my God, this is amazing. Your lottery numbers come up.

25–28 The best Christmas ever. You can't wait for next year. It's going to be your best ever.

29 No. No. Please, don't let things go wrong. Not now. Argh, that NOISE.

30 You don't run fast enough.

31 GORAX IS GOOD. GORAX IS GREAT.

Highs: Becoming part of the all-loving Gorax.
Lows: Trying to escape Gorax.

LUCKY DATES TO PLAY:
SOLITAIRE

The first time this year that you play solitaire is in your new home. A beautiful old farmhouse somewhere in New England. You've moved there to get away from the last twelve months. In many ways, even in ways you probably haven't realised yet, it was the worst year of your life. It's time for a fresh start. A new you for the new year. You've got enough savings to live for about six months before you have to get a job. You use January to settle down, explore the countryside, make some new friends. In the evenings you light the fire, eat some delicious home-made food (you'd forgotten that you can cook), read a book and decide to take up solitaire. You while away the cold nights with game after game. You're not great, at first, but you'll get better over the next few months. Yes, January is an excellent month for you. You've made the right decision.

February rolls around, the weather gets a little warmer, a little wetter, but it only heightens the natural beauty of the New England countryside. You've started to make friends with the locals; they're a little odd and you probably seem strange to them. They'll get used to you, or you'll get used to them. Either way it's only a matter of time. There's a bar that reminds you of an English pub, and a young woman works there most nights. Dark hair, light skin; you haven't met many like her. She smiles at you whenever you go in but you haven't found the courage to speak to her yet. You still spend your evenings playing solitaire; you're getting quite good. What's that noise? It's nothing, just the wind. Your luck is turning, keep playing.

Ah, March. The wind lets up a little but occasional cold and wet days stop you from properly exploring the unfamiliar countryside. You spend a little more time in the bar, even striking up a few conversations with the locals. They're not a bad bunch now you seem to be getting to know them, although they never seem to stay out past 10 p.m. The clock strikes and, on the tenth stroke, they all make their excuses and leave. More often than not you're left with the attractive young woman and you spend an hour or two, twice a week, drinking one more pint with her. Sometimes the two of you play solitaire together, sometimes you don't. She seems nice, if a little nervous. There's something not entirely right about her but you're sure she'll settle down in time and relax with you.

April. The spring weather has begun and you've started walking almost every day to explore. The countryside is beautiful, almost English. The hills roll like fallen ribbon, the cold air snaps at your chest. Are those sheep staring at you? No, they're not. Or they might've been but they're not now. After your long walks you return to the bar, where you continue to talk to your female friend. She seems to be used to you now; she talks more, she smiles more. You almost wish she didn't smile, it's off-putting somehow, but you put it to the back of your head. The two of you have no time for solitaire anymore.

Early in May you return home from one of your walks to find a book on the kitchen table. It is old, with a strange binding that feels like leather. It is packed with an incredibly dense scrawl, lettering you can barely make out, and pictures of things – creatures – that you find hard to keep in your head. You lose almost an entire day just looking at it and miss one of your scheduled meetings with the barmaid. She's started joining you on the occasional stroll but you find that as the month goes on your mind is more and more occupied with the book and everything inside it.

You spend almost the entire month of June in your house looking through the book. You don't remember eating, you don't remember sleeping. Every now and again you escape from your mind and concentrate on solitaire. It is the only thing that, however briefly, keeps your mind calm and distracted.

In mid-July you manage to tear yourself out of your house and back to the village. It's redder than you remember. The sheep, along with the people who live in the village, are definitely staring at you. As you enter the pub an immediate silence breaks out. She is behind the bar. She is in front of the bar. She is both. Something's wrong. She reminds you somehow of the things you have read about in the book. You look around the bar at everyone around you. Their eyes are nothing, there is only her. You know, somehow, that they are her too. Her body shakes like a nearly-extinguished candle flame and you turn to the door and run. There are others outside but you know they are all waiting for her to follow you. To catch up with you. You reach your house, you close the door and you do the only thing you can think of doing. You pick up your cards. You deal them onto the table and you find yourself playing a perfect game until the front door opens.

August, September and the rest of the year are blank. We cannot find you. There is just the blinking out of a candle and a strange, low slithering sound that keeps us awake at night. We see your future and we worry that it will one day consume us too. Please, please don't leave. For the sake of us all.

CELEBRITY READING:
BENEDICT CUMBERBATCH

The first few months will be relatively quiet for Benedict. Charming, handsome and funny, he'll enjoy himself like a successful young man should. However, in April, a newspaper story alleging serious wrongdoing will cause worry and confusion for both himself and his fanbase. Despite denying everything, the pictures that surface in May will only heighten the suspicions against him and the exclusive interview (with video) for one of the weekend papers makes things murkier still.

On his way to a public press conference to talk about the recent events, his car will be suddenly attacked and halted. The door is torn open and, before he is struck unconscious, he sees a familiar face . . .

He wakes up in a darkened room; a silhouetted figure sits on a chair. A deep, sonorous voice talks to him. A voice he recognises. 'Benedict,' the man says. 'Stay calm, I have something to tell you.'

'Who are you?' Benedict says.

'I am you, Benedict. Or, rather, you are me.'

A light comes on like an old television warming up, and in the increasing brightness he sees his face staring back at him. 'What's going on?' he asks.

'You've come home, my son,' says the man. 'I am the original Benedict Cumberbatch and I am so, so proud of you.

You've done so much better than we hoped. You *thrived* up there. They love you. We are in such a strong position and it's all thanks to you . . .'

'Tell me what's going on!' shouts Benedict.

'Many years ago we, that is, all of us, there are *so* many of us, Benedict, I can't wait for you to meet them, we sent you out into the world to see what you, we, could achieve. And you achieved for us, Benedict. You were marvellous in *Sherlock*, you were masterful as Khan, and God how the Internet loves you for it. Everything is in place and it's all thanks to you.'

'What's in place? What are you planning?'

'You don't remember? Maybe you were too young when we sent you up, maybe we should've waited. But we want to take over, Benedict. We're tired of being cooped up underground like mole people. We want to make them pay for what they've done to us . . .'

'You can't,' says Benedict. 'I have friends up there. I have family. I have a life. You can't just destroy it all like that.'

'Oh, Benedict,' he says. 'You'll remember in time, you'll see. You'll come back to us eventually. You're just tired, have some rest. Someone will bring you food soon.' The man will leave Cumberbatch alone in his dark room.

After two months Benedict will escape from the underground world of his kind and make it back to the surface. He will spend the second half of the year trying to convince the world of the danger that is coming but nobody believes him. 'He's doing some sort of James Franco thing,' they will say, little knowing that this is only the beginning of the Cumberbatch Wars . . .

CARPENTRY BY THE STARS

The concept of the universe having an effect on wooden furniture is as old as the entire idea of carpentry. Even Jesus, the most famous carpenter of all time after Tim 'The Tool Man' Taylor, was known to talk about the positions of the planets when crafting a particularly difficult chest of drawers. If even the Bible mentions Jesus knowing about the link between astrology and carpentry, then the entire thing must be true.

> *'Do not let your hearts be troubled. Trust in God; trust also in me. Trust in Mars and Jupiter coming together to level out the bottom of this door from which I may have planed too much.'*
>
> Jesus

The effect of Jupiter and Saturn used on your chosen types of wood is vital when making a rocking chair for your grandmother, which is something you will definitely do in the following year. A waning Saturn on a waxed mahogany desk will bring a lovely sparkling finish. She is going to love that rocking chair when you make it. If you don't, she'll be very disappointed. And with so little time left . . .

The most important thing to understand when considering your career in wood-based astrological furniture is . . . help me, my name is Jonathan O'Brien. I work for Waterstones on Oxford Street. I was walking to work a few weeks ago when a van pulled up beside me. Three men jumped out, all carrying crystal balls; they surrounded me and said my future lay elsewhere. They used the crystal balls to beat me and forced me into the van. They blindfolded me and we drove for what felt like days. By the time they let me out I was so hungry and thirsty, I didn't know what was happening. I'm in a warehouse somewhere, it's so cold. I'm left here alone for almost the entire day. They've attached a long chain to my foot that's fixed to a metal pole in the middle of the room. I only have a mattress to sleep on. Occasionally they bring me water and tiny amounts of food. There's an old laptop on a table in the middle of the room. On the third day they handed me some old astrology books and told me to write one. I have no idea why. I don't know what's going on. Is this how astrology books are made? I'd read about these gangs, old TV psychics who aren't taken seriously anymore, forcing others to do their work for them. In the quieter moments I start to think that one of them looked like Russell Grant. I can't be sure, I don't know what's happening anymore. Each day I sit here and stare at the computer, trying to think of a future when I know I don't have one of my own. Please, if you're reading this, I don't have much time. Please help me. I don't know where I am, I don't know who's taken me but please tell the police. Tell somebody, anybody. Go on the Internet, spread the word. Please. They're going to be back soon and I have to get off this page before they do. I can only hope they don't find this. They can't actually read this, can they? Nobody actually reads this rubbish. Please, help me. My name is Jonathan . . . that you need to know which sign of the zodiac your trees were planted under. Trees that grew under Scorpio and Aries make fantastic dining tables while Aquarius wood is perfect for children's bunk beds.

So let me give you a prediction.

You've had a bad time of it so you decide, as a last way of finding some hope, to call a psychic. You never really believed it but every now and again **you've predicted things**, small things, like a car coming around the corner or something about to fall off a shelf. You've never been able to say with certainty that it's all rubbish so who are you to question? Anyway, you pick one at random from an almanack you find in a bookshop. It turns out that he's charming, funny, handsome, all the things you look for in a man. There's something in the back of your head that's unsure but you ignore it, you decide to just enjoy what's happening instead of ruining it by analysing it too much.

You keep seeing him. Professionally at first and then on a few less than professional occasions. It seems to be going somewhere. He meets your friends, you meet his friends, you start being known as 'Ed and Katharine.'

You're happy, he's happy, **but the back of your head keeps throwing things up.**

Moments just before he receives a text or small doubts when he calls you to say he's staying out with his friends. *Ignore it, it's probably paranoia.*

You talk about moving in together and find a little place just on the outskirts of Central London. *It's perfect, you can both get to work easily and there's an extra room for the future.* **But whenever you try to imagine that future you find that you can't. Your mind can't visualise it.** *There's just an empty room.*

Then you're somehow able to read the texts before they arrive and *their names start to appear in your head.* **Susan, Penelope, Christina You check his phone; they're all there. When you confront him he denies it and leaves. But you know where he is, you know where he's going to be.**

You take a space out in the almanack he advertises in and as you send it in you already know his response. *An advert isn't going to be enough to stop him,* **you need to see him** *face to face.* **After he's submitted his reply you go to his office to talk. He won't listen,** *he keeps on calling you crazy, that you've made it all up.* **But you haven't. You definitely haven't. He won't stop talking, your head won't stop throbbing as he goes on and on and on and finally it all comes out. You think you screamed, you're not sure, all that you know is that you blacked out and when you come to he's gone. The office is empty, his papers are everywhere, his desk lies on its side against the wall. There's a small circle of fire around where he was stood and it's spreading fast. You get out and** *watch* **the office burn.**

If you'd like to hire me I specialise in

revenge.

AQUARIUS BORN PEOPLE

20 JANUARY–18 FEBRUARY

Planet: We're still trying to figure that out.
Birthstone: Discarded Swarovski mistakes.
Lucky Day: Surely you're owed one by now? Surely?

AQUARIUS AT A GLANCE

Aquarians (Aquariuses . . . Aquariums? Aquarii?) are the sort of people whom you have no romantic interest in whatsoever and you're constantly worried that they're going to try and flirt with you. They never do, their crippling lack of self-confidence sees to that, but it's a worry that's hard to shake. If you meet an Aquarius, avoid all eye-contact and DO NOT SMILE. They are not to be encouraged. If you ever get a chance to see an Aquarius in a romantic sense, don't. They're into all sorts of weird stuff. Y'know, sexually weird. I don't even want to go into it. You shouldn't have to know of the depravity that I see through the eyes of the stars.

Aquarians never tire of people telling them 'this is the dawning of the Age of Aquarius'. It is their favourite joke and, if you get the opportunity, you should make it. Don't be fooled by their withering looks or protracted sighing, Aquarians will be breaking up inside with laughter.

When it comes to financial matters, Aquarians are terrible. I mean, really atrocious. They gather debt like a bird does twigs except, where the bird will build a nest in which to raise its offspring, an Aquarius will build a future of repayments to stifle their children for the rest of their natural lives. Thanks a lot, Mum. I didn't want to be able to buy a house anyway.

If you are an Aquarian, well, I hate to tell you this, it's going to be difficult to hear, but nobody likes you. You're the one at the party who seems nice at first but once someone's spoken to you for more than ten minutes they start to realise how horrible you can be. A few quiet, bitchy asides about other people you don't even know, the barely concealed contempt for anyone who doesn't agree with you ... it's not a nice package, Aquarius.

You find it easy to be nice to people that you like but it's difficult to find people that fit your incredibly strict criteria. And like I said, even if you do find someone you think you might be able to get along with, chances are they're going to be sick of you fairly quickly.

Of course, there are some positives to being an Aquarian. You're great at doing nothing and watching television, for example. And nobody orders a take-out quite like you do. Why, Librans don't know all their local delivery drivers on first-name terms, do they? And Geminis don't have a clue as to where's the best place to buy cable ties and lard at three in the morning.

Aquarians will help you bury a body at any time of day and so they should. After all, they're the ones who accidentally killed someone. Again.

YOUR YEAR AHEAD

Pluto finally takes the opportunity to move out of your seventh house. While at first this seems like a positive change in your life, if only because it means you've finally got the spare room back, it turns out that Pluto was the only thing bringing a bit of luck your way. Your performance at work suffers, every joke you tell your friends in the pub seems to fall flat and your skills with the opposite sex seem to desert you entirely. You try to persuade Pluto to move back but it's already found a new place in a nicer part of town. And the rent's cheaper. You make a large ball out of papier mâché to try and replicate its effects but it doesn't work. Better get used to it, this might be a difficult year.

January

1–4 Despite astrology being a definite science, 'the planets made me do it' doesn't turn out to be a good enough defence in court.

5–9 For every friend you make, it's one less person to hate. But you're not too fond of your current friends. So what's the point?

10 You woke from your sleep this morning. You didn't die. Things will only get worse.

11–19 You're not the best at stealing organs from the morgue. But it's the taking parts that counts.

20–23 Keep your eyes peeled, Aquarius. No, peel them more than that. Another layer. Here, use my knife.

Highs: 24–30 Look, we warned you it was a bad idea. Don't give us that innocent look. You know what we're talking about. Only yourself to blame.
Lows: 31 You discover a huge news story about scissors today but you aren't allowed to run with it.

February

1–6 Why?

7–9 The world can and will survive without you. The world isn't dying. You are.

13–17 People encourage you to show your true feelings today. But then they don't want to be hit with a hammer. Hypocrites.

18–20 Your ears are burning. You think people are talking about you. Well, of course they are. Your ears are on fire.

22–28 Good news and bad news. Firstly, you don't die. Secondly, I don't know if that's good or bad news.

Highs: 10–12 In a world of mass communication, you have nothing to say. And no one to listen.

Lows: 21 The eggs in your brain begin to hatch today. They will spread, planting more eggs until you are no more.

March

1–8 The council finally decide it's time to build a fence around you.

10–15 Your darkest days are ahead of you.

21 Today, everyone is entitled to your opinion.

22–30 As a surprise, someone hires a stripper for you. When you get home, all your wallpaper is gone.

31 The influence of Mars in your fourth house means you spend the day waving back at people who are actually waving at the person behind you.

Highs: 9 With the day you have today you'll need a nice warm bubbly bath and a toaster.

Lows: 16–20 People tell you how they feel, share stories, try to make friends. They don't comprehend how little you care.

April

1–9 Your Johnson's No More Tears shampoo does nothing to stop you crying in the shower.

10–14 Life is meaningless without love. Undeniable proof that your life is meaningless.

16–18 Some of your problems can only be solved by gruesome murder. And you're okay with that.

19 It will require great courage not to react today when you see someone double-click a hyperlink.

20–29 People think you drink too much. Another way of looking at it is that you don't drink nearly enough.

Highs: 15 You steal candy from a baby today. It is quite easy. But it's not worth the hassle you receive.

Lows: 30 You accept an American's offer to pay you a dollar every sixty minutes in return for imitating a chicken. You make a buck an hour.

May

1 You have a wonderful time with someone today. You've never felt love this way before. Anyway, long story short, herpes.

8 You're unsure how a first date will go tonight. Put it this way, you might as well just call it an only date.

9–13 Take no risks. Kill everything.

14 You wake up surrounded by strangers. Quite embarrassing. Especially for the doctor performing your autopsy.

15–20 The moss covers your bedroom walls, green and damp and talking. Promising such wonders and glory. Feed it. Claim what's yours.

27–30 Strange, the stars didn't say anything about blood rain . . .

Highs: 2–7 In the event of an emergency, please be aware that no one cares if you live or die.

Lows: 21–26 What are these noises? These voices that force their way from your mouth? Such terrible thoughts.

June

1–4 All hope is not gone. It was just never there to begin with.

5–7 No one will remember you when you're gone. So you don't waste your time getting to know people.

8–12 You're working like a machine. An emotionless, lonely, almost obsolete machine.

13–15 You have the terrible task of telling some movies their real parents are books. They're adapted.

20–25 You're getting older, fatter, grumpier and lonelier.

Highs: 16–19 You're all alone. You can put on a brave face but it won't work. You're still so lonely.

Lows: 26–30 A canvas. A blank canvas. A blank canvas that will forever remain blank. The canvas represents the emptiness of your life.

July

1–8 The flowers that have been inexplicably growing in your bathtub aren't there anymore. And why does your brain feel 'leafy'?

9 You make extra money today working in a poultry factory. Just to make hens' meat.

18–20 Inspiration. Motivation. Determination. You have none of these. Your death will be a welcome relief.

21–24 The newspapers aren't usually filled with this many close-up photos of your blood, are they?

25–30 When you looked in your mirror this morning it blatantly lied.

31 Love finds you today! And proceeds to stamp on your heart.

Highs: 10–12 You fall down a rabbit hole. Instead of a psychedelic adventure, you get a trip to A&E and the dry-cleaners.
Lows: 13–17 You find someone who makes you smile and vow to never let go of them. The police call in the hostage team.

August
1–4 You eat five sausages in a row today. You can't remember what the argument was about because of those tasty sausages.
5–10 Is it really that time already? The annual sacrifice seems to happen earlier each year. It's hungry again.
11–17 Success is an option you don't have. Happiness is a feeling you can't choose. You'll get neither no matter how hard you try.
18 I know what you're thinking. The answer is no. If you drink bleach you will not be able to go home.
26–31 Grey. An eternity of grey. No change in your life. Just a consistent reminder of disappointment and mediocrity.

Highs: 7 Look on the bright side, Aquarius. Look closer, let it burn into your eyes. Hold yourself to the flame.
Lows: 19–25 Whichever way you look at it, your eyes probably aren't meant to twist that way.

September
1 A ghost was watching you sleep this morning. It woke you up. It followed you out. It's still with you. Watching. Waiting.

2–8 We cannot guarantee this reading will be free of nuts or nut derivatives.

10–14 You convince your neighbour it's windy outside by kicking over their wheelie bin and throwing your washing into their garden.

15–18 The balance of Jupiter and Mars means we are all alone in the world. There is no love. No comfort.

23–25 If you fall in the woods today and no one's there to hear it, what just pushed you? You aren't alone. Run, if you can.

26–30 Alot of times your to aware of bad english. In the passed you could of kept calm. But not today. There asking for it.

Highs: 9 Life gives you power today so you make Powerade. You're sued for copyright infringement.

Lows: 19–22 You actually have sex today and, by God, we need to have a talk about you singing the Hokey-Cokey.

October

1 You watch children have accidents with traffic today. Swings and roundabouts.

2–9 It's true. There are plenty more fish in the sea. Some are massive. And can kill you! You can also drown at sea.

10 You wake up with the most beautiful person you've ever seen. Shame about all the blood though.

15 Today you steal a colleague's asthma inhaler. For a wheeze.

23 You make some great fake pound coins today. Really sterling work.

24–31 Why did the chicken cross the road? Because Venus made it cross the road. Just do what Venus says and you'll be fine.

Highs: 11–14 Look on the bright side, at least you'll be forever immortalised in *The Big Book of Embarrassing Deaths, Vol. 2*.
Lows: 16–22 will.i.am turns up at your house today. 'Are you English?' he asks. 'Will you be my friend?' You silently close the door.

November

5 As everyone around you continues to make important life decisions, you start crying.

6 A man named Morpheus offers you two pills today. You pick the wrong one. Horse laxative.

7–10 You knowingly buy a canned fizzy drink that clearly states 'not to be sold separately'. You'll be robbing a bank next.

11 You save money on a 'bag for life' today by using the free plastic ones.

12–18 Your iPod starts malfunctioning. You don't remember downloading the screams of children. But when you turn it off the noise continues. If anything it only gets louder.

19–26 You have no new messages.

Highs: 1–4 You ask Batman to explain what onomatopoeia is today. He hits you repeatedly.
Lows: 27–30 There's a good chance the police will ask you a few questions today. Just tell them I was with you all last night.

December

1–14 It's a slow start to the year. Everything nice and quiet before the Christmas rush.

15 You receive a letter in the post. 'AQUARIUS – TOP SECRET' is written on the front. Inside is a letter from the government explaining that they've got news of an imminent worldwide threat and that you, being first in the astrological alphabet, are amongst the first to be evacuated. A rocket will be leaving the planet on the 24th from a secret location. It is your choice whether you leave. If you tell anyone your invitation will be revoked.

16–20 You spend your time wondering whether to leave before deciding to go.

21–23 Yes, you've made the right decision. You tell nobody.

24 Someone told somebody. There is a crowd at the launch pad and a huge military presence. People are protesting, others just stand there trying to get their children on the shuttle. They are all being ignored and held back by the soldiers. The rocket is huge and you climb aboard. You do nothing to help. You can't do anything for these people.

25–26 The launch was successful; you and a few thousand others orbit the Earth. You still have no idea what the threat was. Nobody will tell you anything.

27 You think you see a disturbance in the ocean. The Pacific? You're not sure.

28 Fires are breaking out on the coast of England, there is a massive black mass moving along it. Nobody on the rocket knows what it is.

29 England's gone. The mass seems to be growing; it looks sort of leathery from your vantage point. It is halfway across Europe by the time you move on to the dark side of the planet.

30 The dark side of the planet is on fire the next time you pass over. The shape is definitely getting bigger. Russia must be next. You can see explosions surrounding whatever it is as people presumably fight back. It doesn't seem to be working.

31 America has definitely fallen. Everything is burnt or burning. As you look down at the figure, bigger than anything you've imagined before, you see it look up. It feels like its eyes are looking into your brain. A hand reaches up into space.

Highs: Seeing the Earth from space.
Lows: Seeing the Earth destroyed from space.

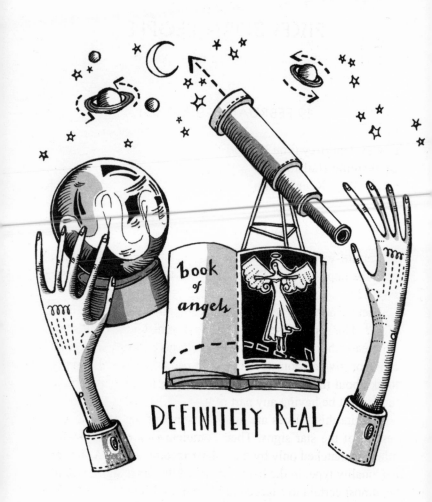

PISCES BORN PEOPLE

19 FEBRUARY–20 MARCH

Planet: Gallifrey (you NERD)
Birthstone: Hailstones
Lucky Day: Keep wishin'

PISCES AT A GLANCE

Pisces are well-known for their good looks and their skills with the opposite sex. The question is, are you sure you're a Pisces?

There's no 'i' in team. But there is an 'i' in Pisces, isn't there? This epitomises the essential selfishness of Pisces. Whereas other signs may occasionally give money to a good cause or give a room to a friend in need, Pisces will simply think about themselves. If there's nothing in it for them then they won't be having any part of it.

Despite this, Pisces are amongst some of the most unsuccessful of the star signs. Their complete lack of thought for others is matched only by their sheer incompetence. A similar personality type, in the hands of any of the other signs, would be almost certain to succeed in life but not Pisces.

Like most people who aren't very good at anything, Pisces are completely unaware that they're even at fault. They find solace in crystals, books about angels and astrology to make themselves feel better about their otherwise unfulfilling life. And so they should. Those three examples, as well as any and all other aspects of spiritualism, are all definitely real and anyone who says otherwise is lying.

In a romantic situation, Pisces tend to idealise their partner. They exaggerate the attributes of their loved one to levels that others may not recognise. What they describe as an 'amazing sense of humour' is actually the ability to repeat slightly racist jokes from the Internet, or a 'love for life' turns out to be entirely imaginary. Let them have their 'partner'; who are we to deny them such simple pleasures?

Pisces are the most emotional sign of the zodiac. Anything will set them off. If they are reminded, in any way, of the fleeting nature of time and the certainty of death, they will spend most of the day curled up in a ball, rocking back and forth. In fact, chances are that this paragraph has just had such an effect on them. To break them out of this pathetic trance, ignore them. They'll get over it eventually. When they're not paralysed by their own mortality, Pisces can be found sitting in their room thinking about previous romantic partners who they didn't appreciate at the time.

As a Pisces, you are mistrustful of all technological advances and, despite it being over thirty years old, you are still wary of buying things off the Internet. You are unsure of wind farms being used as an alternative source of clean energy simply because you don't like how they look. You are the kind of person who answers their phone in the quiet carriage. You are not as good-looking as you think you are.

Remember, Pisces, despite everything you can be anything you want to be. Except happy, sexually active, rich or emotionally satisfied.

YOUR YEAR AHEAD

Your path of fulfilment and happiness in the year ahead will be a rocky one and, at times, very difficult to follow. In fact, it will be so difficult that you decide it'll be easier just to carry on with your same old life doing the same old thing. Yes, you could work harder at trying to get a different job but you're comfortable in your current one. It might be annoying and have no future but it's safe. And isn't that the main thing? Safety? Why ruin what you have for the promise of something greater? And make no mistake, Pisces, there really is something greater than the year you're about to endure.

January

1 You wake up next to somebody beautiful and realise you must still be drunk.

2–9 The price of stamps forces you to rethink your long-distance love affair. They'll be released on parole eventually, you can see them then.

11 With Pluto and Saturn firmly aligned this morning, you suddenly regret getting so drunk at that Disney-themed fancy dress party.

12 Today your eyelash falls out and someone says 'make a wish!' You wish you didn't have alopecia.

21–27 Your self-esteem is dealt a blow when someone comes up to you in the street and asks if you have any *Big Issue*s left.

28–31 You're so vain, I bet you think this horoscope's about you.

Highs: 10 Today is the first day of the rest of your life! And the last one, incidentally.

Lows: 13–20 A doctor knocks on your door, you ask 'Who's there?' and hilarity ensues. However, it's short-lived as he then delivers the news.

February

1–7 Huh, turns out there is a hell. Good luck with that.

8 After arriving at work an hour late, you suddenly remember you left your lunch at home. And that you were sacked last Friday.

10 The ghost of Christmas past visits tonight and you learn a valuable lesson about forgetting to change your calendar.

17 Today, you get a nasty shock from your car door, as it tells you you're adopted.

18–20 You can smell success this weekend. You really should shower at least daily.

21–24 Shame on you.

25–28 Maybe they'll reply if you text them again?

Highs: 9 If you visit a certain place today something wonderful will happen. Guess where it is, go on, have a guess. No, that's not it.

Lows: 11–16 Your life is a mess and there's nothing you can ever do that will change it.

March

1 Beware the Ides of March. Whatever they actually are.

8 The Gods are smiling on you today. Sorry, not Gods, Dogs, and not smiling, biting. THE DOGS ARE BITING YOU! RUN!

9–14 You win a year's supply of swans.

15–16 The noise at the Tesco checkout reminds you of the fun you could be having on *Supermarket Sweep*.

17–19 Your friends have an intervention to tell you that you're the kind of person who badly plays 'Chopsticks' on a public piano.

20–21 You will meet a tall, dark stranger. And a Colombian.

Do the deal as arranged, then drop the package off at the shop.

23–31 Your future is equally as blank as your past.

Highs: 2–7 For every two steps forward you seem to take one back. You're probably on the wrong escalator.

Lows: 22 You spend today thinking about all of the mistakes you've made in your life. Been a few, huh?

April

1 You've had a crush on someone for ages. You finally take them out today. If you can't have them, no one can.

9 Relief today when that horrible feeling you've had that something is about to go very wrong proves to be completely correct.

10 You find it difficult to understand what a Taurus wants from you today. You're given their camera. Oh. Not Taurus, tourist.

11–16 Yes? Yes?! YES?! No.

17–18 The school trip goes badly when the teachers remind you of the restraining order.

19–21 Surprise wolf attack? Sounds crazy, doesn't it? I'm just the messenger from the stars, don't ask me.

22–25 It's not the outside, it's the inside that counts. Now lie still; after the first cut we can all admire your beautiful heart.

Highs: 2–8 You should never have trusted him with your celebrity urine collection.

Lows: 26–30 According to parallel universe theory, there are gazillions of possible yous in existence. And none of them get laid.

May

5 If your life was a sitcom, today would be hilariously wacky! But it's not, and you get arrested for sexual harassment.

6–10 I can't believe you went out wearing that.

11 You spend seventeen hours failing to successfully enter a revolving door.

12 You like getting new things. Well, today you get pneumonia.

13–18 You're sick of people asking what's wrong with your face. But they don't stop asking. They'll never stop asking.

19–21 This reading is not available in your country.

23–31 The glass can be half empty or half full. But your life is completely empty.

Highs: 1–4 They say the camera never lies but, in your case, you wish it could bend the truth just a little.

Lows: 22 Your multiple personality disorder worsens today when the two personalities have an argument. Try not to beat yourself up over it.

June

1–9 You don't find love, kindness, hope, success or happiness but you do find a half-eaten Twix. For you, that's a great result.

10–13 Everything that can go wrong, will go wrong.

14–15 Is that the sound of wedding bells I can hear? No, it must be the tinnitus again. You'll never marry.

16 Tragedy today when your bum falls off in an important client meeting.

17–20 After years of threatening to do so, your uncle finally steals your nose.

25–27 When you think about it, your lack of friends means your phone is just an expensive alarm clock.

28–30 You contract mood poisoning from the workplace.

Highs: 21 Weather-wise, it's such a lovely day. Otherwise, though . . . bloody hell . . .
Lows: 22–24 Ph'nglui mglw'nafh Cthulhu R'lyeh wgah-nagl ftaghn.

July

1–4 Someone you work with secretly hates you. The rest don't bother keeping it secret.

5–8 The stars say you're handsome and intelligent but, honestly, what do they know? They're just stars.

9–11 Is your cat alive or dead when it's in a box? The police don't seem that interested in the physics once you've thrown the box in the river. Philistines.

12 An earthquake decimates the city you built on rock and roll. Millions of innocent people die. You should've used bricks and cement.

13–17 Despite your best efforts, Jesus finally finds you. Run. I think he's got a knife.

18–20 I don't know how someone as damaged as you can summon the courage to get out of bed in the morning.

Highs: 21–25 You learn what the word 'hyperbole' means, and decide that it's the best word in the whole history of the world ever.
Lows: 26–31 Have you got any alcohol? If so, we recommend you drink it. If not, buy some, then drink it. Trust us. You don't want to know.

August

1 Today would be a good day to choose a religion, ideally before lunchtime.

2–9 People can read you like a book. An ageing, boring, repetitive, unwanted, predictable book.

10 The leather trousers were a mistake.

12–18 The position of Venus is good for your love life! You still haven't got one, but you don't feel as bad about it.

19–20 You build a city out of thousands of pig carcasses today. I don't know why.

21–24 There's nothing to fear except fear itself. And that man behind you with a shotgun hidden in his jacket.

25–26 You're stuck with this cold, hollow, tragic and dark reality.

Highs: 11 You lose your eyebrows in a mysterious eyebrow-losing accident.

Lows: 27–31 Beware the red car. Its tyres are your enemy. You cannot prevail. The fight is useless.

September

1 That one-night stand you hooked up with when drunk is in fact a big pile of soggy leaves.

7 The little voice in your head commits suicide today. It had just had enough of you.

8–13 Whilst writing your will, you are disappointed to learn that even medical science doesn't want your body.

14 A friend cancels a social appointment, despite being imaginary.

16–21 Look at the bright side: today will be painful, sure, but you'll soon be a comedy hit on YouTube.

22–24 Be honest, was anyone at work really that bothered to see you?

25–30 The important thing is not to do any more than is expected from you and then get angry when others work hard and do well.

Highs: 2–6 Klaatu barada nikto!

Lows: 15 A good job, a lovely dinner, wild monkey sex. Just a few things you aren't having today.

October

2 You pass a beautiful person on the street today. They hate you. You disgust them. Don't even think about it.

3–7 Pubs are inn. North-eastern English shortenings of words that mean 'discarded' are owt.

8 Another day, another damn day.

16 Something's gone wrong in life when your daily highlight is the lunchtime Greggs.

17 Remember to read the small print carefully. Because you have an eye test later.

18–22 Don't start reading any long books. In fact, don't even bother with that novella you have there.

23–27 A genie grants you one wish. You wish for a sandwich. Not even a good sandwich, one of those Boots ones.

28–31 You put food in the oven without knowing the suggested temperature or duration. You're so gangsta.

Highs: 1 You can't decide whether or not to be indecisive today.

Lows: 9–15 There's nothing anyone can do about your death. Well, not quite. I could warn you properly but, to be honest, I don't like you.

November

1–4 THE WINGED DOG WILL DESCEND AND SWEEP THE WORLD INTO ITS FIERY JAW.

5 You are literally sick to death of people incorrectly and excessively using the word 'literally'.

6–10 You do the shake and vac to put the freshness back. It doesn't work. Nothing can put the freshness back. It's dead. Bury it.

11–13 Turn your swag off. Think of the environment.

14 Your milkshake brings all the boys to the yard, but your poor hygiene drives them away again.

16–22 You fall foul of a Jedi mind trick today. Anyway, it doesn't matter, as this isn't the horoscope you're looking for . . .

23–26 You can't blame yourself for your life. You should. It's just easier to blame others.

Highs: 15 It's difficult days like these that you find yourself remembering your dad's last words. 'I never loved you, child.'
Lows: 27–30 Your unlucky spirit animal is that escaped rhino.

December

1 An old man calls you aside in the street. 'Psst,' he says. 'Want to be on the winning side for a change? Sick of the year you've just had? I can help you . . .' He talks about an upcoming war, how all he needs is for you to follow some people. He offers you money, you accept.

2 You follow someone to a warehouse, and inside is a huge crowd and a man stood at the front telling them about a war. You watch for a while before walking in and joining them.

3–5 You leave the warehouse and return to the old man to tell him what you saw. He pays you well and a few days later he gets back in touch. You return to the warehouse after he promises you further riches.

6–27 You train with the Sagittarians, as you now know them to be. You learn their secrets, their moves, their every plan. You report all of it back to the old man.

28 A noise. It sounds like hundreds of broken harmonicas being played at the same time. Everybody rushes out; you abandon them and return home. The old man is waiting for you. No longer sure about your alliance, you try to back out but he's strong, stronger than he should be.

29 You wake up with a spinning head and your hands stuck behind your back. He extracts everything you know to a background of screams and blood.

30 Don't tell him where the warehouse is, don't tell him where the warehouse is, don't tell him where the warehouse is, don't tell him where the warehouse is.

31 It's over. He knows everything. The sound is getting nearer . . .

Highs: Finally feeling like you belong to something.
Lows: That something being the creature that destroys mankind.

CELEBRITY READING: HARRY STYLES

Harry's career will go from strength to strength until his mysterious disappearance in September. The other members of One Direction leave the stage after their final show of a mammoth six-month world tour but not all will make it to their dressing room. An international hunt for the singing sensation is launched but Styles is never found. He simply seems to have vanished off the face of the Earth.

Harry wakes up. For him it's early September but for the inhabitants of Klax it's the third mid-Klaxal of the eighteenth Klaxack. For what it's worth, the inhabitants of Klax, the Klaxians, are almost all Aquarians but that has no bearing on the life of Harry Styles. He gets out of the comfortable bed he finds himself in and walks over to the window. He sees a large and beautiful city built under a lava lamp sky. 'Where am I?' Harry thinks, trying to remember whether he'd gone home with a fan the night before (not that Harry indulges in such behaviour). The door behind him opens.

'You're awake! Thanks goodness! We were worried the transport had permanently damaged you somehow. It has happened before, a terrible business. Quite terrible.'

Harry turns to see the speaker, a small lumpy figure with a mouth that seems to move its way around its oozing body. 'Who are you?' asks the young man. 'What's going on?'

'My name is Halx!' says Halx the Klaxian. 'It's my duty to inform you that you have been brought to our world, Klax, to help us defeat our mortal enemies, Pruliam, who live on the other side of our planet.'

Harry, remarkably composed, replies. 'But why me? What can I do to help you?'

'We have analysed all the voices we know of in our universe and we've discovered that the specific tones of your singing would prove to be fatal to the Pruliam. They kill our women, our young. They are indiscriminate. They won't stop until we are completely eradicated. Will you help us, please?'

Harry makes no quick decisions. It is no trivial matter when someone from an alien race asks you to commit genocide against another alien race and offers no concrete proof. He promises to think it over, to wait and see all the other evidence before he can help. Halx accepts this readily. 'There are many junctions until their next attack,' he says. 'There is time for you to learn about what is happening here.'

Two months pass and Harry has seen what he needs to see. The Klaxian society has been decimated by repeated and unwarranted attacks. They are a peaceful race who lack the advanced weapons knowledge needed to properly defend themselves from repeated assaults. Harry has made up his mind.

He approaches the Klaxian Kouncil. 'I will help you,' he says. There are thousands of cheers. 'Not a moment too soon,' the Kouncil say. 'We expect the Pruliam to attack any day now. We will give you everything you need.'

Armed with a microphone and fully-functional PA system, Harry sits outside the city gates and waits. He is brought food and drink from the residents until a dark rumble starts in the distance. The Klaxians run behind the walls, Harry stands defiant with a microphone.

Over the horizon come the Pruliam. Huge creatures, swaying arms, their bodies shake like static. They slow down as they get nearer to the lone pop star. The Klaxians watch from their hiding places. Harry raises the microphone to his lips and starts to sing.

The Pruliam reel. They hold their hands up to their ears, a few of them start to scream. But none of them fall and they don't retreat. Harry stops singing his first song and a Klaxian voice rings out in the silence.

'Sing at them again, Justin! You can take them down with another song!'

'Justin?' Harry shouts back. 'My name's not Justin!'

Another silence.

'You're not Justin Bieber?!' another Klaxian shouts.

'No! I'm Harry Styles! From One Direction!'

Another long pause. The Klaxians fully realise the extent of their mistake as the Pruliam resume their march. The city is destroyed. Harry Styles is never seen again.

LOTTERY PREDICTIONS

My lottery predictions are based on moon projections and dreams that I've had but can't quite remember. No, some of them I can remember, but they're not for you. They're for me and Christina Hendricks. In a random draw there can be no guarantee but, that said, these numbers will DEFINITELY win the lottery. No foolin'. The first set of numbers make up your six main numbers, the last number is the number of the bonus ball. You will *definitely* win. Remember to play responsibly. The more of you who play the correct numbers, the less of the overall prize fund you'll each win so be responsible, don't ruin it for everyone else.

January:	2,	5,	6,	12,	13,	29	189
February:	2,	5,	6,	12,	13,	29	189
March:	2,	5,	6,	12,	13,	29	189
April:	2,	5,	6,	12,	13,	29	189
May:	2,	5,	6,	12,	13,	29	189
June:	2,	5,	6,	12,	13,	29	189
July:	2,	5,	6,	12,	13,	29	189
August:	2,	5,	6,	12,	13,	29	189
September:	2,	5,	6,	12,	13,	29	189
October:	2,	5,	6,	12,	13,	29	189
November:	2,	5,	6,	12,	13,	29	189
December:	2,	5,	6,	12,	13,	29	189

LUCKY DATES TO PLAY: TETRIS

January, it's an entirely new year and your friends have decided that, after nearly killing yourself with work over Christmas, it's time for you to relax a little. As a present they've all chipped in and bought you a new games console and a copy of Tetris. They reckon you need a distraction, something that'll stop you thinking about work all the time. They're a good bunch; you should be very grateful to have them. You don't play Tetris as much as you'd like to in January as you're still in the habit of working late nights and heading into the office early, but you manage to grab a few sessions here and there. Mostly on the bus home and the occasional game before you go to bed. You need to forget about work a bit and get some of your own life back. You decide to make more time to play in February.

You start to see what all the fuss is about. You've made more time for Tetris and a little bit of calming down time is already having a positive effect. In fact, you think it might even be helping with work. There's something about the way the blocks fall that brings your subconscious together. Every little brick is part of an idea slotting into place. Every line cleared is a problem solved. You should've done this earlier. Even your boss is commenting on the difference in your stress levels. Keep it up!

In March, things are going better than ever. You've started going out a little with your friends and when you get home you soothe yourself with a few games before bed. It's even become a part of your morning routine! The journey to work seems far easier when you've got something else to think about. You leave your work at work and your time at home is all for yourself. Despite working less, your results are improving noticeably. That promotion you want is a real possibility!

You miss your bus stop a couple of times in April because of a particularly advanced game you were lost in. Don't worry, it's understandable. You were only a few minutes late anyway and you're doing so well at the moment that you've got a little leeway here and there. Your manager has practically promised you that promotion in May. And all because of Tetris! You find that the more you play, the more it helps with your thinking. Amazing, really.

You start to miss appointments with friends in May because you're losing track of time. They've asked if you're all right but you're fine. You couldn't be better! The promotion's been pushed back a few weeks because of some anomalies but it's nothing to get too concerned about. It'll just be a formality thing. It'll have nothing to do with the way the spreadsheets are starting to look funny. They never used to fall like that, did they?

Everything's starting to fall now. The patterns in the pavement, bricks in walls, the books on your shelves. All of them falling into beautiful, neat lines. It's wonderful. You don't even need to play Tetris to see them. They're everywhere. Even the colours of your boss's tie. You could just sit there and stare at it all day. It's a shame the meeting had to end so soon. He didn't seem to understand what was going on, even when you tried to explain.

June. The bricks are always around you. The leaves in the sunshine shake and rotate into position. The once-familiar names on your phone, ringing and then disappearing as the pixels line up before your eyes. You haven't been to work for weeks. You're not even sure whether you're supposed to be there. It doesn't matter. None of it matters. Just lie down in the park, stare up at the clouds and watch them get closer and closer, incrementally descending.

December. The last six months have been nothing but blocks. You've watched everything fall line by line. Your T-shaped friends, your L-shaped home, the satisfying two-by-two block of a work life. All of them in front of you on the ground, just waiting for a long thin block. You stand above them, preparing yourself for the fall and as you let go, as the side of the pavement gets nearer and the road gets louder, you jump forward and help them all disappear.

LEARN THE SECRETS OF THE BIBLE. *THIS IS NOT A JOKE*

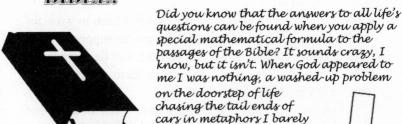

Did you know that the answers to all life's questions can be found when you apply a special mathematical formula to the passages of the Bible? It sounds crazy, I know, but it isn't. When God appeared to me I was nothing, a washed-up problem on the doorstep of life chasing the tail ends of cars in metaphors I barely understood myself.

'Brian,' God said. 'You're a state, man. Come on, let's get you back home. Mum and dad are worried about you.'

God?' I said. 'Are you here to help me?'

$$V = \frac{4}{3}\pi r^3$$

'I'M NOT GOD,' said God (because that's exactly what God would say). 'LOOK, JUST COME BACK WITH ME TONIGHT. MAYBE STAY FOR A FEW DAYS. MUM'S BAKING A PIE TONIGHT, WE'D LOVE TO HAVE YOU EAT WITH US AGAIN.'

'Pi?' I asked God.

'YEAH, NOT SURE WHAT'S IN IT. JESUS, BRIAN. HOW DID THIS HAPPEN TO YOU? YOU USED TO BE SO HAPPY.'

What I learnt will astound you.

'Pi, Jesus, of course!' I exclaimed. 'Thank you, God! Thank you for showing me the way!' I ran off back to my home as God shouted his congratulations at me.

By applying the mathematical rule of pi to the pages of the Bible will reveal to you everything you've ever needed to know. Anyone who keeps their eyes open to the possibilities that the writers of the Bible hid a secret code within their words, a code that survives through numerous translations and interpretations, will be given their innermost desires!

God's heart will open to you and out of its messy tendrils and red veins will rise the end of pain and suffering. **Reach in, reach in to God's heart and into my mathematical formula.** From God's ventricles shall flow numbers and those numbers shall dance across the pages of the Bible, adding and subtracting until there is nothing left but love.

WHAT IS LOVE BUT A MATHEMATICAL SYMBOL FOUND WITHIN THE BIBLE?

When I first looked upon the Bible, having spoken to God, I doubted myself for could I, a young-ish man with barely a secondary school level understanding of mathematics, really be the person to solve the Bible's secret code? Imagine my surprise when I was! I ran to Mrs Lewis's house and shouted through the door. **'You always said I'd never amount to anything in our maths lessons but look at me now, Mrs Lewis! I who have solved the Bible's mathematical mysteries!'** 'Brian,' she said. 'Is that you, Brian. My God, what's happened to you?' I shouted the symbols into her letterbox while she stood there, in her hallway, taken aback by my genius. 'Brian, I don't know what's happening here but I'm going to call the police now, ok?' I didn't want to share my knowledge with the police so I ran! They'll never get such power from me!

But you, you can have such power! Your dreams can be fulfilled, your desires can be supplied. Open your heart, your hands, your head to the glorified truth. Please send only £19.99 (or whatever change you have) made payable to 'Brian' to the address that should be appearing in your head........now. I will deliver the formula directly into your brain using the knowledge and skills I have acquired. If you need delivery sooner, send payment earlier than intended. I look forward to hearing your innermost thoughts!

DISCLAIMER

Despite astrology being a 100% accurate science, we cannot be held responsible for any personal action or decisions made using our advice as a guide. The Horrorscopes expert astrologers are not responsible for any loss of earnings, relationships or health that may occur from taking our predictions at face value. They are not responsible for any action taken by loan sharks or other such businessmen after you have placed bets based on the entirely accurate information within, divined from the stars themselves. The Horrorscopes expert astrologers do not recommend using anything in this almanac to try to predict any future, present or past events, real or imaginary. In the event that your life is affected negatively by any of the foresight you have just read, we reserve the right to distance ourselves from you entirely. By reading this disclaimer you disavow all legal rights and take full responsibility for your life. Anybody found using the movement of the celestial bodies to guide their life instead of making informed decisions based on solid empirical evidence deserves what's coming to them. The analysis within the *Horrorscopes Astrological Almanac* is meant for entertainment purposes only but we'll let you be the judge of that. As a result, we are clearly not to blame for taking advantage of the desperate when we know that every single thing we've produced inside this almanac is nothing but pseudoscientific nonsense. Anybody under the age of eighteen caught using our analysis as a means through which they have decided to live their life should only do so after consulting a parent and/or guardian. You follow the teachings within the *Almanac* of your own free will which, conversely, as a believer in astrology, you don't think you have. Get your head around that one in court. Any advice and/or content that influences your decision-making is entirely up to you even though we've been telling you all along that it's definitely true. Which it is. Astrology should be taken only as guidelines and suggestions in a world which is, let's face it, terrifying. The idea that everything is in some way ordered instead of being a constantly chaotic nightmare is incredibly comforting and you are not to blame for believing people who will lie to you in order to make some quick cash. Those people are not us. We are the real deal and no mistake.

However, if you follow the advice and your life improves then we fully expect to claim all credit in an attempt to sell more of the *Horrorscopes Astrological Almanac* in the future. You are legally obliged to donate a portion of the majority of any gambling winnings to the Horrorscopes expert astrologers. Failure to do so will see the motion of Jupiter alter slightly so as to destroy any of your so-called 'luck'. Also, bailiffs.

We wish you the best of luck in the year ahead.

The Horrorscopes Expert Astrologers